STATE SHAREHOLDING

Also By Richard Minns

The Organisation of Housing: Public and Private Enterprise in London
  (*with M. Harloe and R. Issacharoff*)

STATE SHAREHOLDING

The Role of Local and Regional Authorities

RICHARD MINNS
and
JENNIFER THORNLEY

First published 1978 by
THE MACMILLAN PRESS LTD
London and Basingstoke

*Associated companies in Delhi
Dublin Hong Kong Johannesburg Lagos
Melbourne New York Singapore Tokyo*

*Printed in Hong Kong by
Dai Nippon Printing Co (H.K.) Ltd*

British Library Cataloguing in Publication Data

Minns, Richard
  State shareholding.
  1. Stockholders – Great Britain   2. Local
  finance – Great Britain
  I. Title   II. Thornley, Jennifer
  332.6'725   HG5432

  ISBN 0 – 333 – 23739 – 0

Contents

Preface and Acknowledgements

This book is the result of a research project on shareholding by local and regional authorities which was largely funded by the Social Science Research Council. During the course of our research the number of authorities acquiring shares in companies grew and when we completed our research the number seemed likely to grow further.

Our research began in May 1975 and finished in July 1977. We examined all the local authority shareholding schemes in Britain. Amongst the regional authorities, we examined the shareholding of the Highlands and Islands Development Board in detail; the Scottish and Welsh Development Agencies were only established during the course of our research and by the time we completed our work these agencies had not really begun theirs; the Northern Ireland Finance Corporation/Northern Ireland Development Agency could not be examined in the same detail as the Highlands and Islands Development Board because of our own resource limitations of time and money. We relied on interviews with individuals involved in the various schemes as well as with others in central authorities, with lawyers, accountants, and others. We also examined company reports and accounts.

We were able to present preliminary ideas and papers on our work at conferences and seminars at Aston University, York University, Oxford University, Warwick University, and in published articles. We are very grateful for the help and criticism we have received. We should also like to thank in particular Michael Ball, Richard Barras, Alex Catalano, David Donnison, David Eversley, Margie Jaffe, Doreen Massey, Brian McLoughlin, Enzo Mingione, Bill Morrison and Andrew Thornley for comments, criticism or other help at various stages of our work. In addition, we are especially grateful to the countless individuals involved in the shareholding schemes who gave freely of their time when we approached them for information. Finally, we should like to express our thanks to our secretary and typist, Barbara Freeman.

vii

List of Abbreviations

CDA	Comprehensive Development Area
CoSIRA	Council for Small Industries in Rural Areas
DLO	Direct Labour Organisation
ECI	Equity Capital for Industry
GLC	Greater London Council
GMC	Greater Manchester Council
HIDB	Highlands and Islands Development Board
ICFC	Industrial, Commercial and Financial Corporation
IDC	Industrial Development Certificate
IRC	Industrial Reorganisation Corporation
LDS	Locally Determined Schemes
LUT	Lancashire United Transport Ltd
MEB	Municipal Enterprise Board
MMC	Manchester Mortgage Corporation Ltd
NBC	National Bus Company
NEB	National Enterprise Board
NEC	National Exhibition Centre
NIDA	Northern Ireland Development Agency
NIFC	Northern Ireland Finance Corporation
NRDC	National Research Development Corporation
PAG	Planning Advisory Group
PTE	Passenger Transport Executive
QUAGO	Quasi-governmental organisations
QUANGO	Quasi-non-governmental organisations
REB	Regional Enterprise Board
SDA	Scottish Development Agency
SELNEC	South-East Lancashire/North-East Cheshire
SIC	Shetland Islands Council
SVA	Sullom Voe Association Ltd
SVEAG	Sullom Voe Environmental Advisory Group
TWG	Technical Working Group
WDA	Welsh Development Agency

Introduction

State shareholding by local and regional authorities is an entirely new phenomenon. Over the last ten years local councils and regional authorities have acquired shares in public and private companies. Between 1968 and 1976 there were 20 companies in which 10 local authorities owned shares, 15 companies in which the 8 local authority Passenger Transport Executives (PTEs) owned shares, 23 companies in which the Highlands and Islands Development Board (HIDB) owned shares, and 17 companies in which the Northern Ireland Finance Corporation (NIFC) owned shares. There was therefore a total of 75 companies in which local and regional authorities acquired shares in this period.

The number of companies in which local and regional authorities own shares is still small. Nevertheless, the total amount of private capital involved in many of them has been very large. Where development projects have been concerned some companies in which local authorities owned shares were involved with projects of major national importance. For instance, local authorities have become involved in schemes which are part of or have assisted in the development, extraction and processing of North Sea oil, the construction of the largest shopping centre in Britain, the construction of Britain's National Exhibition Centre and Britain's biggest conference centre, and the planning of London's third airport. Similarly, where local and regional authorities have owned shares in companies, large investment by national or multi-national companies has been involved; in the case of regional authorities these companies included Shell, Wimpey, Fitch Lovell and Booker McConnell; in the case of local authorities the companies included Prudential Assurance, Rio-Tinto-Zinc, Town & City Properties, John Mowlem & Co., Whitbreads, Guinness Mahon, Grand Metropolitan Hotels and Cadbury Schweppes.

The small number of cases where local and regional shareholding has occurred must also be seen in the light of the attempts by the authorities to gain legal powers for this purpose. Between 1965 and 1973 38 local authorities individually obtained legal powers in local Acts of Parliament enabling them to acquire shares in companies for the purpose of land development. Subsequently the Department of the Environment announced that private Act powers were no longer necessary for this and that a power to carry out ancillary activities, contained in the 1972 Local Government Act, would suffice. In transportation, as well as land development, it has been relatively straightforward for shareholding powers to be extended to the local level.

Where non-development (manufacturing and commercial) companies are concerned, various general Act powers have been used for shareholding purposes. For instance, South Yorkshire County Council launched a scheme to subscribe for shares in certain firms operating in its area by using a part of its staff pension fund. Nottinghamshire County Council used a supplementary power of a general Act in order to acquire shares in a company. This supplementary power allowed it to spend a proportion of its ratepayers' money in the general interests of its area. However, the adequacy of this power has remained unclear. Some local authorities have continued to explore the extent to which it can be used, while others, such as Tyne and Wear and West Midlands County Councils have tried to obtain local Act powers specifically for shareholding purposes. The attempts to obtain local powers have, on the whole, not been successful and as a result of the legal situation there are few examples of shareholding by local authorities for non-development purposes.

In contrast, powers have been granted to the Scottish and Welsh Development Agencies and to the HIDB and NIFC specifically for shareholding purposes. This has provoked discussion amongst a number of local authorities concerning the formation of a regional agency with similar powers for the North of England. Also, various authorities have started to discuss joint schemes with the National Enterprise Board enabling national government shareholding to take place in consultation with local authorities.

Shareholdings have been acquired by the national level of the state for decades but the nature and *scale* of this has altered since the mid-1960s with the establishment of the Industrial Reorganisation Corporation (IRC) in 1966, and the National Enterprise Board (NEB) in 1975. These agencies both had powers to acquire shares in companies. It appears that there is a link between what has occurred at the national level since the mid-1960s and what has occurred at the local and regional levels. More work has been done examining state shareholding by central authorities than state shareholding by local and regional authorities. Interesting questions can be raised about what part these developments at local and regional levels have played in the overall development of the role of the state over the last decade. Shareholding at these levels can involve public authorities in the management of private enterprises, and in making profits from commercial ventures. This is very different from the traditional role that local and regional authorities have played in Britain since 1945. We need to consider how shareholding has emerged out of this traditional role.

Shareholding has been used increasingly for national, regional and local 'planning' purposes. Figure 1 indicates the traditional 'planning' role of national, regional and local authorities as well as national, regional and local shareholding activities. At national level shareholding has been used as part of national economic 'planning', at regional level for regional

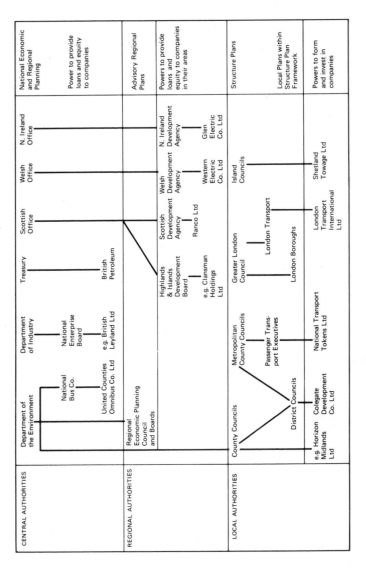

FIGURE 1   National, regional and local authorities: economic and land-use 'planning' (as of 1977)

The vertical lines in the Figure represent only a partial and variable indication of the lines of policy control. Some are left out, such as the control of the Treasury over aspects of other central, regional and local authorities, and some are very weak, such as the control of County and Metropolitan County Councils over District Councils in their area. It must be taken for granted that the Treasury has a pervasive influence because of its control over the raising of state revenue.

economic 'planning', at local level for local land-use 'planning' and other
ad hoc economic purposes. Economic and land-use planning' are two kinds
of 'planning' which are frequently considered as separate processes. Land-
use 'planning' is usually associated with local authorities, while economic
'planning' is usually associated with national authorities. Regional
authorities are associated with both land-use and economic 'planning' at
different times. The Figure shows how weak the links are between these
activities at different levels of government.[1] The sections of Figure 1 which
primarily concern us at this stage are those on local and regional
authorities. The section on national authorities concerns us only in so far as
it affects local and regional authorities.

Local land-use and regional economic/land-use planning have traditionally been negative and weak when compared with the type of state
intervention introduced at the local and regional levels from the mid-1960s
onwards. At the local level, the basis of British land-use planning was
founded shortly after the Second World War, following a series of official
reports commissioned by the government containing recommendations on
various aspects of town planning. These reports – known as the Scott,
Uthwatt, Abercombie, Reith, Dower and Hobhouse Reports – were
prepared between 1941 and 1947 and created the context for the ensuing
legislation.

The 1947 Town and Country Planning Act was concerned primarily
with the land-use allocation of post-war development activity. It assigned
to local authorities the power and the duty to prepare Development Plans
for their areas, showing in detail the proposed uses of land and the stages by
which the development of land should be carried out over twenty years.
Within this framework local authorities were empowered to grant
planning permissions for development or changes of use. These planning
permissions were the means by which plans would be implemented. This
system was largely negative in that the role of local authorities was to
respond to events and processes in accordance with the Development Plans.

An important exception to this was the New Towns Act of 1946 and the
Town Development Act of 1952 which gave special new town authorities
and expanding town councils the initiative in various fields of development. These authorities were, however, few in number and were geared
mainly to generating public sector development in locations which would
provide alternative growth centres to London and other large
conurbations.

The Development Plans system was reviewed between 1964 and 1965 by
the Planning Advisory Group (PAG)[2], resulting in the 1968 and 1971
Town and Country Planning Acts. The outcome of these Acts was a new
Development Plans system under which 'structure' and 'local' plans were
to be prepared by local authorities, producing overall a more flexible
planning process based on a more rigorous planning procedure. The
Structure Plan was to be a written statement of policy which:

should cover the context of national and regional policy and local circumstances in which the plan has been prepared, the objectives of the plan and the reasoning behind the full explanation of the proposed overall strategy and its component policies and general proposals, including their relationship to each other and to the likely availability of resources.[3]

The Written Statement was to be backed up by key diagrams, surveys, population, housing, employment and other forecasts, analysis of issues, alternative policies and evaluation, and be subject to a monitoring procedure. Within this framework local plans were to be prepared where necessary giving detailed land-use proposals. No change was recommended for the development control procedure by PAG or introduced by the 1968 and 1971 Acts. In other words, despite the development of a much elaborated plan-making system with a considerably widened scope of inquiry, no increased powers were made available to implement the new plans. It was assumed that the existing development control system was adequate and that the function of local authorities was to respond to development and investment initiatives made by the private sector.

Between 1947 and 1975 three attempts were made to give local authorities power to intervene in the land market. However, none of these were concerned to give local authorities power to initiate development on the land. The 1947 Act contained provisions to compensate all landowners for lost development rights at the market price of land excluding any gain accruing from its development potential, and to charge a betterment levy on developers who enjoyed financial gain from any development. However, this system depended on the continued operation of the private land market, while at the same time removing any incentive for private development. The result was a 'drying-up' of the land market. In 1953 the new Conservative Government abolished the betterment levy and reduced payment of compensation to the cases where landowners had applied for and been refused planning permission, and in 1959 compensation for land compulsorily purchased was changed to full market value including development gain.

In 1967 the Land Commission Act was passed by a Labour Government enabling a Land Commission to buy up land for future development purposes and for a betterment levy to be paid whenever land changed hands. The Act failed for similar reasons to the 1947 Act and its provisions were rescinded by an incoming Conservative Government in 1970. Finally, in 1975 the Community Land Act was passed empowering local authorities to buy land themselves at market value and, under the 1977 Development Land Tax Act, to charge a development land tax on the private sale of land, (i.e. a proportion to increase over time of the difference between base or market value and market value including development gain).

In summary, land-use planning by local authorities in Britain since the Second World War has focused attention on plan-*making* and the *allocation* of development and investment by the public and private sectors. Where the public sector was concerned it has been able to allocate local authority capital investments within the constraints of the land market and borrowing powers. Where the private sector was concerned, the negative form of implementation powers has meant it has been *reactive and responsive*.

The one outstanding exception to this was in local transport planning which is regarded as an integral part of land-use planning. In 1968 transport planning was reorganised at national, regional and local levels, with the establishment of public corporations with positive planning powers at the national level (the National Bus Company and the National Freight Corporation), and special Passenger Transport Executives at the local level, also with positive planning and implementation powers which included shareholding in companies 'for the purposes of the business of the Executive'. PTEs later became an integral part of local government.

This coincided with the use of shareholding for planning purposes by local authorities. Local authority shareholding enables planning at the local level to be a more positive activity. Ownership of shares allows an authority directly to influence all aspects of the functioning of an individual private firm – land and building needs, financial needs and manpower needs. Shareholding does not change the structure of the private firm or assimilate it into the public sector.

The same problems of negativeness and weakness in the traditional system of local land-use planning apply at the regional level of planning and to national economic planning, so far as it affects the regional level. Most regional economic and land-use planning has been the responsibility of central authorities. Before 1965 regional land-use plans were produced by central government departments (e.g. the *South-East Study*, 1964). In addition, policies towards the 'assisted areas', as they are called, are a central authority responsibility. The 'assisted areas' include Scotland, Northern Ireland, Wales, Northern and South-West England and have experienced higher than average unemployment rates. They receive additional state expenditure in the form of additional industrial investment grants and (from 1967 to 1976, and later for Northern Ireland), employment grants, as well as extra selective financial assistance for particular projects. A scheme of Industrial Development Certificates is also operated by central authorities. IDCs are a negative control over the construction of new industrial premises outside the assisted areas. However, nine out of ten applications for IDCs are granted even in the South-East of England, and it is estimated that only about 15 per cent of the companies refused IDCs in the South-East or the Midlands eventually invest in the assisted areas. IDC negative controls operated by central authorities have not improved the employment situation of the assisted areas relative to the rest of the country.

In 1965 the government introduced a system for developing regional planning and coordinating it with national economic planning. A Department of Economic Affairs at the national level, responsible for drawing up a National Plan, was complemented by Regional Economic Planning Councils (appointed by central government) and Regional Economic Planning Boards (of civil servants). The Councils had no executive powers but were responsible for preparing regional plans. The structure started to collapse when the British economy failed to grow as fast as the plans assumed. The regional plans also concentrated heavily on physical or land-use planning as commonly understood, especially in the South-East, rather than on economic planning.[4] The main responsibilities for regional planning subsequently passed to what became the Department of the Environment, while the longer-term economic planning functions were transferred to the Treasury; subsequently what became the Department of Industry assumed some of the medium and long-term economic planning functions.

After 1970 regional plans were no longer produced. Other regional land-use plans and documents were written by joint bodies of local authorities, such as the Joint Planning Team for the North-West, the Standing Conference on London and South-East Regional Planning, the South-East Joint Planning Team, and the Northern Region Strategy Team. These sometimes included the Department of the Environment and contributions from the Regional Economic Planning Councils. Some dealt with economic planning issues more than others. But this planning system had shifted away from a systematic link between national and regional economic planning coordinated by a central economic planning authority towards a dichotomous system of economic planning for the country and regions at the national level, while local authorities and their joint bodies provided the regional/local land-use planning machinery, partly involving a central non-economic planning authority – the Department of the Environment.

This structure reflected the different approaches to regional planning by local and central authorities respectively:

> What central government means by 'regional planning' is primarily the correction of economic imbalance between one 'region' and another; and it is only with reluctance that central government is reconciling itself to the fact that this purpose – crucial to its central function in the economic field – necessarily involves the making of investment decisions within 'regions' on a territorial as well as a functional basis. What local government means by 'regional planning', on the other hand, is primarily the expression of national policies in terms of a comprehensive long-term strategy for economic and physical development within each provincial-scale 'region', in the context of which local planning authorities can work out meaningful structure plans for their own areas.[5]

Regional planning was also carried out by various agencies at the regional level with executive powers set up by central government: the Scottish Industrial Estates Corporation, which was responsible for the government's factory-building programme in Scotland, and the Welsh Corporation which was responsible in Wales. There were also the Rural Industries Bureau and the Rural Industries Loan Fund, which operated as the regional agents in England and Wales of the Development Commission, an organisation set up in 1921 to provide credit for small firms in rural areas; the Small Industries Council for Rural Areas of Scotland was the Commission's agent in Scotland. In 1968 the Rural Industries Bureau and the Loan Fund were consolidated into the Council for Small Industries in Rural Areas (CoSIRA) and in 1971 a similar body was established in Northern Ireland called the Local Enterprise Development Unit.

However, the most significant development in regional economic planning over the last ten years or so has been the establishment by central government of separate public corporations in some of the regions: the Highlands and Islands Development Board (1965) and the Scottish Development Agency (1975) in Scotland, the Welsh Development Agency (1975) in Wales, and the Northern Ireland Finance Corporation (1972, becoming the Northern Ireland Development Agency in 1975) in Northern Ireland. The SDA incorporated the Scottish Industrial Estates Corporation and the Small Industries Council for Rural Areas in Scotland (SICRAS): the WDA incorporated the Welsh Industrial Estates Corporation and the Welsh section of the Council for Small Industries in Rural Areas (CoSIRA).

The HIDB, SDA, WDA and NIFC/NIDA reflect a different approach to the regional economic planning which had predominated before in four ways. Firstly, they are more concerned to intervene directly in the local economy than to prepare plans. Secondly, the institutions are concerned more with regional economic planning *within* regions. Thirdly, the latest corporations (SDA, WDA and NIDA) are part of a *national* industrial strategy involving the National Enterprise Board. Lastly, the institutions involve central government in devolving executive powers to separate regional agencies on a much larger scale than ever before.

The primary objectives of these agencies are:

helping to establish an improved industrial structure upon which a sounder economy can be developed, improving the profitability and efficiency of industry and increasing employment, [NIFC]; economic and social development of the area through the creation and maintenance of viable enterprises, [HIDB]; the promotion of industrial development and employment by the encouragement and establishment of new enterprise; acting as an investment bank to industry in the area and undertaking joint commercial ventures, [SDA and WDA].[6]

These objectives involved regional institutions in the operations of *individual* firms on an extensive scale. This was similar to the developments at the local authority level we described earlier and to the parallel developments already referred to at the national level in the late 1960s with the Industrial Reorganisation Corporation, which have been described at some length elsewhere. The IRC and related policies represented the end of national level 'indicative planning', which was a generalised policy tool aimed at industry or sectors as a whole, and the beginning of *selective* intervention which discriminated between firms within sectors.[7]

Why did this fundamental change in state intervention occur, what are its implications for the role of the state, and what part will local and regional authorities play in this? We identify three groups of work dealing with the changing nature of state intervention which could be used to explain state shareholding at different levels.

1 QUASI-NON-GOVERNMENTAL AND QUASI-GOVERNMENTAL ORGANISATIONS (QUANGOS AND QUAGOS)

QUANGOs and QUAGOs are special bodies which, it is argued, are not G (governmental organisations) or NG (non-government). They include the Industrial Reorganisation Corporation, the Highlands and Islands Development Board, the National Research Development Corporation, the Horse Race Betting Levy Board, the Regional Hospital Boards, companies in which there are state shareholdings, the Social Science Research Council, the Jockey Club and the Community Development Projects. In fact, there are allegedly hundreds, if not thousands, of QUANGOs and QUAGOs. Their development 'sprang from the need for piecemeal adjustment to radical change in politics, economies, society and culture. . . . The pressing need was to solve new problems by new expedients'. The organisations form a growing part of a 'confusing system' which is neither capitalism nor socialism but which 'jogs along, extemporizing from day-to-day'.[8]

QUANGOs and QUAGOs are said to:

(a) 'buffer' certain activities from political interference;
(b) get round organisational and capability weaknesses of 'traditional government';
(c) help to spread power;
(d) intervene without creating more civil servants, and
(e) support many large organisations which are essential to economic or social life, but which can only survive if taken over by government.[9]

The literature on QUANGOs and QUAGOs concentrates on the organisational implications of these new institutions and discusses these in

terms of the problems they raise for public accountability. 'Deviousness
may sometimes have resulted' in the operation of QUANGOs and
QUAGOs, 'but it was rarely the initial intention'.[10] 'The fundamental
issue is whether governments have the capacity to adapt democratic
institutions to the complex and varied tasks required of the modern state
without sacrificing public accountability.'[11] The theoretical development
of the concept of QUANGO is thus related to the growing 'complexity' of
society. The basic problem which QUANGOs are then seen to create is a
tension between public and private interests that government tries to
resolve by various processes of accountability.

2 OVERLOADED GOVERNMENT

According to this argument, central government has been forced into a
situation where it can no longer deliver what people want.[12] People's
expectations of government's capability have risen as economic performance is increasingly seen as subject to the influence of government, and as
both major political parties compete for votes with promises they cannot
fulfil. The problem also lies in the concentration of decision-making
powers in a single central agency, the British government. It has become
difficult for one agency to reconcile the conflicting demands increasingly
put upon it by the growing number of issues which 'rising expectations and
the increasing complexity and interdependence of society' put upon it.
Interdependence, for instance, means that unions (such as the National
Union of Mineworkers in 1974) can affect the survival of Governments
because, in this case, the British economy had become so dependent on
coal.[13]

One way to reduce the load on central government is to devolve power
and responsibility, either upwards to the EEC, or downwards to regional
and local government.[14] Shareholding by local and regional authorities
could be viewed as a response to this problem of overload. A second
solution to central overloading, which is suggested by those who use this
concept, is the spreading of power and responsibility to 'producer groups':
trade unions and industry. This results in the formation of institutions such
as the National Economic Development Council which includes representatives of the Confederation of British Industry and the Trades Union
Congress as well as the British government. It also leads to agreements
being reached between government and unions, such as the 'social
contract' of 1975/7. State shareholding could be viewed similarly as a
'partnership' of decision-making responsibility between the individual
firm and central, regional or local authorities.

3 CORPORATISM

The 'overload' argument stresses that government is becoming more power*less*. 'Corporatism' argues that it is becoming more power*ful*. A currently debated argument about corporatism[15] 'is that the State in Britain is no longer just facilitating, regulating, protecting, supporting or ameliorating private economic activity; it is attempting to control and direct it. It is not, however, trying to appropriate private enterprise'. Instead, there is developing 'an economic system of private ownership and state control', based on four principles of 'unity, order, nationalism and success'. The important new role of the state is its *direction* of private economic activity. 'The state tells private business what it must do and may not do.' It controls 'the internal decision-making of privately owned businesses'. 'The state does not just attempt to influence decisions, *it prescribes or limits the range of choice open to capitalist owners or managers.*' (Our emphasis.)

This directive role of the state is coming about because of four structural conditions: industrial concentration, declining profitability, technological development, and international competition. 'The corporatist response to the problems [these] create is being precipitated by the current economic crisis.'

The state cannot 'tolerate' profit maximisation with the extremely high level of industrial concentration prevailing in Britain because to do so would be 'to licence corporate plunder'. In addition, the decline of overall profitability and the decline of companies' retained earnings has forced firms to rely on outside sources of finance, including the government. The Stock Exchange has declined in importance as a source of funds and so bank borrowings have risen and 'a stream of companies have been going to the government for emergency assistance'. This has been accompanied by relaxation of price controls by the state in exchange for specific reinvestment obligations by companies. As a result the state takes over and replaces the normal market mechanisms because of the 'anarchic' nature of these mechanisms.

There is a parallel intolerance for the 'anarchy' of the labour market. The state attempts to overcome the excesses of high unemployment as well as the excesses of free collective bargaining in which the unions 'hold the nation to ransom'.

To sum up, according to the four goals of corporatism:

(a) *order* is achieved in the organisation of labour *and* capital by controlling excesses of exploitation by either side;

(b) the corporatist state achieves *unity* by substituting cooperation for competition: this 'goal' arises out of 'a revulsion against the perceived wastefulness of competitive struggles on all fronts: the inflationary pursuit of sectional economic interests, class

divisiveness . . . sectarian bombings, Celtic fissiparousness . . .
home buyers gazumping up house prices, or "extremism" of any
complexion';

(c) *nationalism* is 'the elevation of "general welfare" to complete
priority over self-interest or sectional advantage';

(d) *success* means 'giving conscious direction to the economy . . . the
control and concentration of investment and of the allocation of
resources'.

'Let us not mince words. Corporatism is fascism with a human face.'

The various explanations for the increase in state intervention over
recent years, outlined above, attribute different degrees of importance to
the operation of capitalism in Britain. Sometimes it is referred to simply as
'the economy'. Some give only passing reference to it; the corporatist
argument gives it more importance than the others. It seems impossible to
consider the state intervention that we have been referring to without
looking at 'the economy', and impossible to consider the British economy
without using a rigorous theory of capitalism which can account for certain
developments over the last decade or so. In this book we shall therefore
explore the extent to which a fourth explanatory approach can account for
the processes with which we are concerned. There is no catchword such as
'QUANGOs' or 'Corporatism' which can summarise this approach. It
involves a firm understanding of the functions of the state in the economy,
and an analysis of the particular determinants of state shareholding at the
sub-national levels – the local and regional levels. This will enable us to
explain the development of new instruments of local and regional
'planning' and predict what their future potential and limitations are for
state intervention. It will also enable us to examine the conflicts with, and
relationship to, intervention by central authorities, and also to examine the
implications of shareholding for local and regional authorities themselves.
We will be able to see more clearly the weaknesses in the other three
approaches.

In the chapters that follow we will deal firstly with the economic
developments since 1966, the nature of past local intervention in firms and
development projects, and the history of state enterprise. We will then
move on to analyse local and regional shareholding in more detail;
examining the functions that it performs in state intervention by local and
regional authorities. The concluding section will present our overall
interpretation of state shareholding by local and regional authorities and
will show why we reject the explanations presented in the theories and
concepts outlined earlier.

Part I
The Foundations of State Enterprise

1 Intervention and the Crisis

This chapter will examine the crisis of the British economy since the mid-1960s. It will concentrate on three elements of the crisis which have influenced the emergence of local and regional shareholding: firstly, the restructuring of British industry, and the role the state has played in this; secondly, the 'property boom', and the role the state has played in this, too; and thirdly, the pressures by central government to reduce state expenditure. We will then go on to look at the spatial implications of these elements of the crisis; in other words, we will look at how far they have affected different parts of the country differentially.

Before doing so, however, we must briefly define some key concepts which this chapter will introduce and which will be of crucial importance for our analysis of local and regional authority shareholding.

I DEFINITION OF KEY CONCEPTS

(A) ACCUMULATION OF CAPITAL

Capitalism is concerned with the production and appropriation of 'surplus-value'.[1] Surplus-value is the difference between the value of labour-power contained in a commodity (including the value of labour-power contained in the raw materials and machinery used up) and the total value of the commodity. The value of labour-power is the value of the means of subsistence (historically and 'morally' determined) and training which is necessary for the maintenance, production and reproduction of workers. Only labour can produce value and only labour can produce surplus-value. The process in essence is concerned with the production of value over and above what it takes to maintain labour-power.

The extent to which the rate of surplus-value can be increased depends on the production time available, the degree of labour productivity and the degree of training or skill needed. Labour productivity has increasingly assumed more importance. Various kinds of machinery and mechanisation increase labour productivity; this in turn means that more commodities can be produced relative to the same amount of labour-power. As a result less value is transferred to each commodity, so making each one cheaper. This lowers the value of commodities the labourer needs for subsistence, lowers the degree of average skill needed to produce a commodity, lowers the value of machinery, and so on. In order to sustain the process of accumulation of surplus-value, some surplus-value must be reconverted into capital for use in the production process, i.e. it cannot just be spent on consumption but must be capitalised. Employing surplus-value as capital, then converting further surplus-value which is produced into capital, is the *accumulation of capital*. Accumulation has adopted particular money forms at the level of the company which are relevant to our analysis.

Companies are legally governed by their shareholders, who hold the ordinary shares or equity. The shareholders have risked their money-capital in order to see it expand in the accumulation process. They will be paid dividends out of non-reconverted surplus-value. Their major gain ('capital gain') should be the expansion of their capital in the form of the rise in the price of their shares, reflecting the increased surplus-value which forms the enhanced productive capital of the company. Surplus-value which is converted back into productive capital to continue the accumulation process is referred to as shareholders' funds, internal funds or retained earnings. Should the company collapse, the shareholders may well receive nothing back since their money-capital advanced may have been used up in paying for commodities (including labour-power) in the production process.

Companies can gain credit in various money forms in order to help the accumulation process; the chief one is loan capital. Loan capital, unlike share capital, usually has a fixed annual charge or rate of interest attached to it. It is also usually secured on company assets in order to ensure repayment should the company collapse. Loans are raised for short-, medium- or long-term periods. Bank overdraft facilities can provide additional short-term (and in some cases, particularly for smaller companies, medium- and long-term) finance.

(B) PRODUCTIVE LABOUR AND PRODUCTIVE EXPENDITURE

Productive labour is that which produces surplus-value. It is labour exchanged with capital to produce surplus-value. Surplus-value reconverted into capital for production is called *productive capital*. Capital spent on labour and materials to produce surplus-value is *productive expenditure*.

Unproductive labour is labour exchanged with revenue and does not produce surplus-value. Revenue items include taxes, profits (not reinvested), interest and rent. Most of these revenues are charges on surplus-value; they depend on surplus-value being created by someone else. The revenues become unproductive *expenditures* when they are used to pay for labour or materials. Most state employees are unproductive in this sense because they are paid out of taxes; their services are purchased with revenue whether the taxes are paid out of wages or out of non-capitalized surplus-value; i.e. out of profit, interest, rent. Most state expenditure is therefore unproductive. Although this unproductive state expenditure can help the accumulation process, by training and maintaining the labour force for instance, it is nevertheless a deduction from total surplus-value.

(c) CRISIS

Accumulation is interrupted by crises. Large-scale crises disrupt the accumulation process when insufficient surplus-value is produced relative to capital employed. In a crisis the elements of the accumulation process which determine the rate of surplus-value become exhausted or reach their limits. An overproduction of capital results. When this occurs the rate of profit falls with little interruption from the forces which usually counteract it. Labour is then reduced drastically and capital is centralised and rationalised through mergers at a faster rate than normal, and through the closure of less profitable activities. Capital is reorganised and restructured so that a new cycle of accumulation can begin with an increase in surplus-value relative to capital advanced.

As the rate of profit falls financial institutions will try to protect their investments by increasing interest rates. New loans will be taken on by industry at the higher rate of interest in order to pay off existing financial obligations until the financial institutions realise that no equivalent value has been produced. No more finance will be forthcoming until an increase in surplus-value relative to capital advanced can be brought about. Financial institutions will at the same time attempt to concentrate investment in sectors where value expansion may *appear* more promising. Speculation occurs as credit and loans are advanced on a large scale in these sectors. Eventually it is realised that no real increase in value is occurring in these sectors either. An increase in the rate of surplus-value for capital as a whole can in the long-term only be obtained from a reduction in the level of total capital advanced compared to crisis levels.

II THE BRITISH CRISIS OF ACCUMULATION

We will now discuss three elements of the British crisis of the last decade. These three elements reveal the operation of capital and the state in the crisis.

(A) THE RESTRUCTURING OF CAPITAL

The restructuring of capital results from the falling rate of profit. In Britain the fall in profit rates reached crisis proportions. In 1975 the real rate of return (retained and distributed earnings before interest and tax) on capital employed in large industrial and commercial companies had fallen to 3·9 per cent compared to approximately 12 per cent fifteen years earlier.[2] Internal funds or retained earnings fell from 78 per cent of total capital employed in 1967 to 63 per cent in 1974,[3] and equity issues, which used to provide 12 per cent of new capital in 1955–61, only provided 4 per cent of new funds by 1972.[4] The fall in retained earnings reflected the falling rate of profit. The fall in the proportion of risk capital reflected the unacceptably high nature of the risk because of the inability of industrial capital to generate sufficient surplus-value in relation to capital employed. Loan capital has in consequence risen as a proportion of total capital employed, and the rate of interest on loan capital has increased substantially too. There has also been a particularly marked increase in 'secondary gearing' or bank overdrafts and other higher interest, short-term loans as a percentage of long-term loans; increasing from 63 per cent in the early 1970s to 97 per cent by 1974.[5]

These developments severely affected company financing by over-burdening companies with loan capital, and interest, in relation to risk capital. Risk capital is essential, in some form or other, to companies. If interest payments have to be met on the loan capital then the company may collapse if it exists on insufficient risk capital. Equity, or ordinary share capital, thus performs a buffer role and provides the basis for borrowing.

Companies tried to conserve capital for further accumulation in order to counteract the fall in profit rates and rise in interest rates, by cutting back on dividends to shareholders (distributed earnings). This reduced the attractiveness of risk capital yet further. From 1963 to 1974 dividends dropped from 4 per cent of all personal income to 2 per cent. Shares became very unfavourable investments. They contrasted markedly with interest yields on loan capital. Even when dividends were restricted under the prices and incomes policy, interest payments were at their highest post-war levels.

The restructuring of capital is part of the crisis. As we outlined at the beginning of the chapter, a crisis involves the *reduction* of total capital employed in order to return to an acceptable rate of surplus-value in relation to capital employed. From a peak of £2130m. in 1970 capital expenditure in manufacturing industry moved to £1739m. in 1972, £2024m. in 1974, £1737m. in 1975, and £1660m. in 1976.[6] The takeover and merger of firms is part of this rationalisation and selective reduction of capital. Between 1968 and 1973 large manufacturing firms grew through takeover and merger rather than internal growth and reconversion of surplus-value into productive capital. Most dealings in ordinary shares were share-for-share exchanges in takeover situations.[7] Even the massive flurries of rights issues in 1975/6 (issues by quoted companies of shares to existing shareholders at a preferential price) were intended partly to 'tidy up company balance sheets', and partly to circumvent dividend controls,[8] rather than to generate new productive capital. The least productive firms closed down; other firms were taken over and the least productive parts sold off or closed down. As a result of this capital restructuring, bankruptcy and liquidations increased substantially (from 4298 in 1968 to 7271 in 1975 in the former case, and from 3165 in 1968 to 5398 in 1975 in the case of the latter).[9] These restructuring processes destroy small companies in particular. This is something to which we now devote some attention because of its relevance to local and regional authorities in the restructuring process.

We have described how the rate of interest on loan capital increased as the crisis worsened. Small firms faced this problem particularly severely because of their traditionally heavier reliance on internal funds,[10] which were no longer adequate. They were forced more than usual to turn to outside bodies for financial support. However, small firms found it extremely difficult to obtain outside finance, be it risk capital or loans; they did not have access to the normal capital markets. Large financial institutions, mainly pension funds, insurance companies, unit trusts and so on, have grown to a size where they have come to own approximately 50 per cent of UK quoted shares. It would be unusual for them to invest extensively in small companies. Investment in large firms was easier because the money could be monitored, withdrawn and reinvested fairly simply in significant quantity. Merchant banks, and joint-stock bank subsidiaries, set up since 1970 to provide venture capital for new enterprises, had relatively high thresholds on turnover and profit record which they applied to firms wanting finance. This meant that they rarely dealt with small companies with their lower turnover. The Industrial, Commercial and Financial Corporation (ICFC), a special Bank of England and joint-stock bank consortium set up in 1945 as a concession to small firms by the banks,[11] was prepared to invest medium- and long-term capital in small firms. ICFC was prepared to invest down to £5000 rather than the usual minimum of £30,000 to £50,000, but it tended to invest in what were regarded as untypical, financially secure small firms, and did not invest in *very* small firms with an annual turnover of £50,000 or less.[12]

The problem for small firms in the late 1960s to 1970s should be considered as an extreme case in the historical decline of small firms since the 1930s. Just as large firms have been increasingly producing a larger proportion of total output for decades through concentration and centralisation (internal growth and takeover), so small firms have been declining in their proportion of total output.[13] The 1960s was a period of intensive merger and takeover for large firms, and the beginning of a period of rapid collapse and takeover of small firms as industry as a whole, dominated by large firms, began to restructure and reorganise itself.

Instead of being seen as part of the process of accumulation and crisis, the problem of small firms has traditionally been discussed, in a more

limited way, in terms of whether a 'financial gap' exists for them. The
Macmillan Report of 1931 identified a 'capital gap' for small firms and led
to the establishment of ICFC. In contrast, the Bolton Report of 1971
concluded that although the small firm sector was declining, there was not
any body of 'legitimate unsatisfied demand' for finance; there was no
equivalent to the 'Macmillan gap'. It predicted that the decline in small
firms would level off and leave 'a smaller but still viable small firm sector'.[14]
However, subsequent reports and articles have disputed this. One report
suggested that developments since the Bolton Report did not bear out the
Committee's view that the decline in small firms would level off. It argued
that the sector *was* declining in large measure for financial reasons:

> . . . it has to be admitted that the evidence available to the [Bolton]
> Committee was inconclusive.

The flows of institutional finance and taxation penalised the small firm
heavily. This had serious economic implications:

> The process of concentration has continued long after the technological
> forces underlying it have weakened. . . . The diversion of resources
> away from small firms and towards large . . . reduces the flexibility and
> adaptability of the economy and, related to that, the pace of innovation.
> It does appear that in Britain sufficient numbers of new firms are not
> being formed to perform the function of seeking out and testing new
> products, processes and services to continue the process of economic
> specialisation.[15]

Other reports and articles referred to 'the many small and medium-sized
firms which would have invested more over the past decade if they had had
access to long-term bank finance':[16] others dwelt on the increasing
financial disadvantages facing small firms.[17]

Finally, in 1976 financial institutions set up an equity bank called
Equity Capital for Industry (ECI). The original proposals aimed at
£500m. for ECI, but after extreme reservations had been expressed by
many financial institutions about setting up a fund to assist British
industry[18] the issued share capital was reduced to below £40m. The fund
was designed to invest in 'medium and smaller companies, both public and
private'.[19] In 1977 it invested in its first company. On this occasion one
report commented,

> The problem when ECI was being (painfully) founded was to identify
> areas where the capital markets had failed. Since there was no obvious
> gap such as the Macmillan report uncovered, one had to be
> engineered. Now the one instance where even the opponents of the
> whole project might admit a gap is the case of the company whose
> fundamental situation is sound, but where, because of a kink in profits,
> the capital markets might be unwilling to advance further funds.[20]

This collection of arguments about small firms is not helped by the varying definitions of the small firm sector. Some refer to establishments with fewer than ten employees, the Bolton Report refers to small companies as those with fewer than 200 employees, pre-tax profits of £20,000 or less, and owned by those who manage them. ECI and ICFC include larger enterprises than this when they refer to small firms. For our purposes a small company is one where the owners are the managers of the enterprise. The 'problem' of small companies should not be seen in terms of whether there is a 'financial gap' at the present time, but rather in terms of the extent to which large companies are reorganising themselves at the expense of small companies. This means that we must look at why small firms in particular are closed down or taken over in a crisis, and what the conflicting pressures are for big firms to sustain small firms.

On the one hand, small firms are more labour intensive than big firms.[21] In a crisis the amount of labour employed is drastically reduced so that the value of labour-power can be lowered and the rate of surplus-value can increase, as we described earlier. Since commodities produced by small firms have high labour content, the aggregate rate of surplus-value can be increased by letting a lot of small firms collapse.

On the other hand, small firms perform certain functions for large firms:

1 small companies occupy sectors of limited or variable profitability in a given period and enable large companies to expand into that sector when they choose to do so;
2 small companies pioneer certain new sectors of production at particular times which large companies can take over when the risks are lowered;
3 small companies are also useful for secondary lines of production that do not enter into large-scale, continuous production processes;
4 since small companies are faced with a lower level of labour productivity, their prices are higher; large companies can fix their own prices with reference to those of small companies and gain some surplus profits.[22]

There are, then, certain limited reasons for preserving small enterprises in a large-scale restructuring of capital as a whole. The predominant processes will nevertheless be rationalisation and closure. The role of the state is to support the restructuring of certain profitable firms while the nation's capital and labour employed is reduced.

(B) THE 'PROPERTY BOOM'

We outlined earlier how a crisis contains a tendency for speculation by financial institutions as they try to invest in more 'promising' sectors. The 'property boom' of the 1960s and 1970s was part of this tendency in the crisis and it led to various consequences for the production of surplus-value.

Firstly, most of the available loan capital went into property development rather than manufacturing industry. In 1972/3 lending to manufacturing industry increased by 19 per cent while loans to property companies increased by 75 per cent.[23] Although the 'property boom' of the late 1960s/early 1970s enabled the production of surplus-value for the building companies involved, the enormous rents and leases which could be charged for the completed office blocks represented a growing charge on surplus-value produced elsewhere. The boom involved frequent 'paper revaluations' of properties without there being a comparable number of market transactions. The result was a tremendous growth in 'fictitious capital' with capital apparently doubling itself. The growth in fictitious capital was caused by the unrealised expectations of capital growth; there was no equivalent growth in value produced. The structure of property investment became overstretched, overvalued, and heavily 'geared' (relied on a higher proportion of loans, or fixed interest capital, to risk bearing capital). The expectations of rising value provided security for the refinancing of loans.

The growth in property speculation and the unproductive aspects of it led to the Conservative Government introducing a business rent freeze in 1972. This added to the problems of the property developers. At the same time there were increasing political demands for further controls over property development because of its unproductive aspects. The Conservative Government later proposed a first lettings tax and the Labour Government introduced a development land tax, along with the Community Land Act mentioned earlier. The Labour Government's White Paper on land laid down objectives for achieving an 'effective planning system'. These were

(a) to enable the community to control the development of land in accordance with its needs and priorities; and

(b) to restore to the community the increase in value of land arising from its efforts.[24]

By 1975 the property boom had collapsed and the Labour Government withdrew the commercial rents freeze in order to re-establish an 'orderly market in physical property'.[25]

(C) PRESSURES TO REDUCE STATE EXPENDITURE

We described in the earlier section on unproductive labour expenditure how state employment was an unproductive charge on surplus-value. Increases in state expenditure have helped to exacerbate the crisis.

By 1974 over a quarter of the working population was employed by the

state. Local authority employment by itself rose from $1\frac{1}{4}$m. in 1960 to nearly
3m. in 1975. Social security, health and welfare, education and housing
expenditure had risen to 24.9 per cent of the GNP in 1973 from 17.6 per
cent in 1961. By 1975 the public sector borrowing requirement had risen to
10 per cent of GNP, from 6 per cent in 1973 and 3.6 per cent in 1961.[26] In
order to pay for the increase in expenditure the state had to raise the money
in taxation; taxation also had to pay for the interest on state borrowing (the
public sector borrowing requirement). This then formed an additional
increasing burden on surplus-value produced by industry.

There had in fact been pressure on local authorities, as well as other
public bodies, to reduce expenditure for some time. Central government
attempted to control local authority expenditure in the following ways:

(a) through the control of capital expenditure by the use of loan
    sanction and associated devices. Capital expenditure usually refers
    to school and house building which is carried out by the private
    sector and paid for by the public sector. As we outlined earlier, the
    taxes needed to pay for this are still charges on overall surplus-
    value;

(b) through the control exercised in fixing the level of grant aid to local
    authorities and the exhortations associated with this, i.e. controls
    over revenue expenditure. Revenue expenditure includes expendi-
    ture on social workers, teachers and other unproductive state
    employees. It also includes 'transfer payments' to the old, sick or
    those needing financial assistance with rent payments;

(c) through detailed financial regulation (e.g. external audit).

Loan sanction control over capital expenditure is divided into two main
parts: 'key sector schemes' and 'locally determined schemes'. 'Key sector'
services include education, housing, principal roads, health and social
services, water supply and sewage disposal. Locally determined schemes
(LDS) include those parts of key sector services which do not rank as key
sector and, for example, spending on central area redevelopment including land purchase, land for industrial development, car parking, offices,
shops, sports centres and parks. A third category of capital expenditure,
the acquisition of land for public purposes, is free from loan sanction.
Where the land is bought by the local authority for disposal to the private
sector then permission to borrow the necessary finance is required from
central government. Individual key sector schemes require central
government approval in order that the local authority can proceed with
borrowing money. LDS schemes do not require individual loan sanctions.
Instead local authorities are allocated annual totals of capital expenditure.
The money which can be borrowed under LDS expenditure has been
reduced since 1971/2. In addition, cuts in capital expenditure for housing
were enforced from 1968 as part of the post-1967 devaluation measures.

The most consistent growth in local authority spending has been in revenue expenditure and much of this was due to increases in the proportions of the population eligible under existing welfare programmes.[27] Growth in expenditure was not due to massive new uncontrolled initiatives, but to the fact that there were more unemployed, old people and young people in the population. In 1966 there were cuts in local health and welfare costs as part of the post-election period of economic restraint which led to the 1967 devaluation. After the Conservative Government took office in 1970 there was a further attempt to reduce public expenditure with measures such as the 1972 Housing Finance Act, and the 1971 Education (Milk) Act. The provisions of the latter to withdraw subsidies on school milk for 7–11-year-olds only continued what the previous Labour Government had done to restrict the supply of free school milk. Conflicts between central and local government arose over some of these provisions and one or two local authorities broke the law in order to avoid implementing them, in particular Merthyr Tydfil Council in Wales, Clydebank Council in Scotland, and Clay Cross Council in England. In Clay Cross an external audit led to seven Councillors being 'surcharged' and disqualified from office.

By 1975/6 the Labour Government was announcing cuts in revenue and capital expenditure for a number of services. Nationalised industries also started to reduce their expenditure on labour and capital equipment in 1975. The White Paper on Public Expenditure published in February 1976 provided for a virtual standstill in overall public expenditure for 1976/7. The White Paper stated that the aim was to reduce public spending to 53 per cent of GNP by 1979/80 from a level of around 60 per cent in 1975/6. This meant that certain items would increase to some extent but that there would be substantial cuts in others; for instance, in primary and secondary education from £386m. in 1975/6 to £238m. in 1978/9, in food subsidies from £576m. to £75m., and in hospital building from £378m. to £299m. This was necessary, according to the White Paper, in order that resources of capital and labour would be available for exports and investment. Expenditure items which were not cut included the National Enterprise Board, the Scottish and Welsh Development Agencies, and the Community Land Act provisions for the acquisition of land for development, but these remained relatively small.

We have, therefore, three linked elements of the crisis on which to base further analysis of local and regional shareholding:

(a) the restructuring of capital involving a selective reduction in aggregate capital employed; the need for financial reorganisation of individual firms to ensure a suitable basis of risk capital for future production; the state aiding the restructuring of large firms; a possible or partial conflict between the needs of big firms and those of small firms in which the best long-term interest of capital as a whole is unclear;

(b) financial institutions investing in property development which led to increases in rents and leases as unproductive charges on an already depleted rate of surplus-value; the state trying to influence this;

(c) increases in state expenditure providing a further unproductive charge on declining surplus-value; the state then trying to control this.

The state's role is a pervasive one in all these developments, pulling together the various elements in the crisis in order to facilitate capital restructuring.

III SPATIAL IMPLICATIONS OF THE CRISIS

The spatial or local manifestations of these three elements of the crisis which we now discuss will help us to account for the rise of local and regional authority shareholding.

(A) THE RESTRUCTURING OF CAPITAL

National unemployment increased from 300,000 in 1966 (the end of the mid-1960s recession) to 1·4m. in 1976. Unemployment increased for the first time in decades in inner cities, regardless of the location of the city. Between 1966 and 1975 'the disparities in regional unemployment at standard region level have diminished dramatically. . . . Thus, contrary to past experience, the Assisted Areas are not taking the full brunt of the recession in employment'.[28] This convergence of unemployment rates is similar to that of 1930.[29]

The convergence of regional rates and the decline in employment in what were once prosperous areas, such as London and Birmingham, was often attributed to the successes (and excesses) of regional policy in attracting firms and jobs to the assisted areas. It was argued that if only regional policy could be abandoned, inner city job loss would slow down. An alternative view is that the loss of employment in cities, regardless of area, and the convergence of regional unemployment rates, results from the restructuring process. One study of the restructuring process in the electrical engineering and electronics sectors, found that it was producing more job losses in inner cities than job transfers to new (development area) locations.

Well over half the job losses identified in this study were absolute losses − losses to the economy as a whole. Of these, rather more than half were not involved in any process of locational change − they resulted overwhelmingly from the decline of industries heavily represented in the cities (the kind of loss frequently described as 'structural').[30]

Nevertheless, Development Areas did record a better result (fewer job losses) once the total absolute and locational job losses and gains were calculated. Regional policy could have played a part in this by making certain kinds of mergers and rationalisations easier, but 'if regional policy is not simply regional policy, but is part of the attempt to increase the productivity of industry, and if it is thereby helping create employment problems in inner cities (by helping to shed labour as well as capital), that does not mean one can simply abandon regional policy'.[31] In the electrical engineering and electronics sectors, regional policy and industrial re-structuring helped facilitate a new division of labour and processes between regions, with a small and highly-qualified workforce con-centrated in the rationalised, highly skilled, industrial and research and development activity located in the South-East, and a semi-skilled/unskilled majority working in the restructured, more standardised and less skilled mass-production processes located in the Assisted Areas.[32] This was an indication of the overall processes leading to the convergence in regional unemployment rates.

(b) THE 'PROPERTY BOOM'

During the property boom of the 1960s and early 1970s, large-scale office and town centre development of various kinds took place in most parts of the country. It was not confined to the South-East or the large conurbations.

Oliver Marriott describes a boom in property development starting in the 1950s when the Conservative Government abolished the 100 per cent development/betterment charge introduced by the previous Labour Government. Demand for office space was high because of the destruction of available space caused by war-time bombing, but mainly because of the

> change in emphasis from making goods towards designing and market-ing them, the tendency towards the amalgamation of industry into larger units, and the choice of London for a company's 'prestige' headquarters.[33]

In 1939 in central London there were 89m. square feet of office space. By 1966 the figure was 140m., an increase of 72 per cent.[34]

By the end of the 1960s office building was 'spilling over into the provinces', and the redevelopment of shops 'in High Streets all over the country' was well under way.[35] By 1967 there was about 281m. square feet of office space in Britain. By 1974 there had been a further increase of over 40 per cent to a total of 397m. square feet. The increases for different parts of the country were broadly similar; the percentage increases in each region were at least 32 per cent and at most 56 per cent, with a 39 per cent increase in the South-East, a 36 per cent increase in the West Midlands and a 46 per cent increase in the North-West.[36] At the same time housing construction had slumped from 414,000 units completed in 1968 to 269,000 in 1974.

The result of the speculation in office construction was such that in Bristol nearly 7m. square feet of office space out of a total of 18m. remained unlet in 1976. In the same year in the central area of Nottingham, $\frac{1}{2}$m. square feet was vacant while a further 1m. was 'committed' and under construction. In central Leicester, over 20 per cent out of $5\frac{1}{2}$m. square feet was vacant in 1975; this compared with between 7 per cent and 9 per cent for 1968/71.

Local authorities had become increasingly involved with developments in different parts of the country. The growth in the unproductive nature of office development, with increasing amounts of money being made from rising rents, led to local planning authorities attempting to secure a return 'for the community' where they owned land or when they granted planning permission. In the early 1960s Bradford Council granted a lease for a development in return for an 'undisclosed ground rent'.[37] In the mid-1960s, Blackburn Council also received a ground rent in return for a lease, but, in addition, secured a further percentage of the income from the development by providing for rent reviews under the lease. Many local authorities followed this practice but often provided for very infrequent reviews. Many 'deals' with developers were more trivial, however, such as the provision of land for road space by a developer in exchange for planning permission from the local authority. Notorious examples of this are the Euston Centre and Centre Point developments in central London.

By the late 1960s/early 1970s, local authorities were also sharing in the financing of schemes in exchange for securing part of the financial returns from development and in exchange for being able to influence the nature of the development. They were also using provisions such as Section 52 of the 1971 Town and Country Planning Act to impose certain kinds of minimal conditions on developers. There was increasing doubt about whether the extent, nature and form of property development was desirable. Frequently development schemes that local authorities themselves wanted to encourage to make their areas attractive for further industrial and commercial investment were difficult to implement if there were high infrastructure costs involved or the schemes offered a much lower return on capital.

While local authorities therefore played a small part in attempting to influence the excesses of property speculation the basic processes were beyond their control. After 1972/3 they were faced with a need for a limited amount of controlled development in order to promote investment in their areas, but at the same time they were faced with state expenditure controls over them as part of central government's attempt to restrict certain kinds of unproductive state expenditure.

(C) PRESSURES TO REDUCE STATE EXPENDITURE

We described earlier how there had been a ten-year period of cuts and attempted cuts in local authority expenditure. This affected all local authorities throughout the country and was not restricted to particular areas or cities. There were also cuts in nationalised industry expenditure. These had their effects on certain manufacturers; Post Office cuts affected the demand for the production of telephone equipment, and Central Electricity Generating Board cuts affected the demand for the production of turbo-generators. The effects of these falls in demand are among the items discussed in the earlier section on the regional convergence of unemployment rates. The fall in nationalised industry expenditure only had differential spatial effects in so far as it added to the relative increase in unemployment rates in the non-assisted areas.

There were, however, other cuts in large capital projects which affected different areas. For instance, the expenditure on the third London airport was cut by central government; the government also decided not to make a grant for the development of the 'Picc-Vic' underground line in Manchester. Some schemes were continued, such as the Tyne and Wear Metro system, which we shall describe later; infrastructure provision for the oil development in Shetland was also not affected because of the national importance of Britain's oil supplies. These expenditure decisions were fairly random, depending on how far schemes had already progressed and on other factors. There was therefore no predictable or consistent spatial pattern to them. The only exceptions to this are the regional development agencies, the HIDB, NIFC, SDA and WDA. The cuts did not affect these bodies.

IV THE EMERGENCE OF LOCAL AND REGIONAL
SHAREHOLDING

Local and regional shareholding has emerged as a developing role of the state resulting from these three main elements of the crisis.

(A) REGIONAL AUTHORITY SHAREHOLDING

The HIDB and the NIFC were initially set up as part of a continuing attempt to influence certain political problems in the Highlands and in Northern Ireland. State intervention in the Highlands dates from the rebellions of centuries ago, and in particular the Crofters' War of the 1880s 'and has mainly been justified for non-commercial reasons'.[38] The Parliamentary debates on the establishment of the HIDB in 1965 referred to the continual problems of depopulation. It was argued that industry should be provided to stem the flow: 'to make the Highlands pay we must prime the pump liberally, and persuade Highlanders that the Highlands is a space in which they should stay'.[39] It was concluded that a special organisation was needed:

> My party has continually stated that industry must be spread throughout the country. This requires a national plan. It cannot be done on a purely local basis, by locally elected people. . . . Local councils have been in being for a long time, but have failed completely to do anything for the benefit of the Highlands.[40]

> If we have have a third kind of democracy, regional as well as local and national, we shall find ourselves in a very sad way. It will not be long before other regions demand the same thing, and it will not be long after that before they say that the money provided must be divided among them according to population. When that happens, we can say goodbye to any development in the Highlands.[41]

The NIFC, set up in 1972, resulted from the recommendation of a government-appointed committee that a special institution should be set up to provide substantial financial resources to the private sector of industry. The report 'commented on the danger that the industrial investment momentum, generated in the 1960s, would be lost because of the cumulative effect of civil unrest. This, it considered, justified Northern Ireland being treated as a *special case* for Government aid'.[42]

We described earlier the importance of equity in the capital structure of firms, and how the crisis was reflected in an increasing shortage of risk capital. This affected the activities of the HIDB and NIFC. In 1968 the HIDB indirectly promoted its own Bill to give it powers to acquire shares in companies:

> The object of this Bill is to give the Board and the companies greater flexibility in the management of their capital base.[43]

> I hope . . . that the equity shareholdings will be taken up in *companies which are going to be successful* and will flourish in the Highlands, and that it will not lead to the Board finding itself holding shares in a lot of companies which are failing.[44]

The NIFC was a forerunner of the Scottish and Welsh Development Agencies set up in 1976. The NIFC was itself continued and changed to the Northern Ireland Development Agency. All these bodies may have arisen historically out of the 'non-commercial' ideology of regional policy and were intended to assist 'special cases'. Their main role in practice has been one of playing a part in the restructuring of industry in the UK. Furthermore, as we have already mentioned, the budgets of these regional bodies, though small, have not been affected by expenditure cuts.

(B) LOCAL AUTHORITY SHAREHOLDING FOR LAND DEVELOPMENT

At the local level Table 1.1 shows the local authorities which acquired powers to form companies or subscribe for shares in companies for land development . The relevant clauses of the Acts were fairly similar. They stated that 'the council and any person having an estate or interest in any land' within the local authority's area 'may enter into an agreement' which can determine the order and timing of development. The clauses concluded that,

> The council may take or acquire shares or other securities in any company incorporated in the United Kingdom with which an agreement is entered into under this section.

A Department of the Environment working party had advocated such partnerships in 1972[45] and the government had promised general legislation in 1973.[46] In 1975 the Department of the Environment stated that specific powers were no longer necessary for this kind of activity and that local authorities no longer had to obtain separate provisions in private Acts of Parliament for the purpose of taking or acquiring shares in companies for land development. The participation in companies for land development was judged to be *ancillary* to existing local authority powers. Because it was ancillary it was covered by the local authorities' subsidiary powers, namely Section 111 of the 1972 Local Government Act; this provided that

> a local authority shall have power to do anything . . . which is calculated to facilitate, or is conducive or incidental to, the discharge of any of their functions.

By this time it was becoming evident, because of the post-property boom slump in the land market, that the Community Land Act would not work without some form of state initiative in promoting private capital investment in land development. Finance for the public acquisition of land under the Land Act was quite small, but like the budgets of the regional bodies mentioned earlier, was not cut in the 1976 expenditure proposals. Public expenditure on the *development* of that land, however, was subject to loan sanction control and restrictions as it had been since 1972/3. Local authority shareholding in this period helped to attract and control private capital investment for development purposes, as we shall describe in detail later:

TABLE 1.1   Local authorities with private powers to acquire
shares in companies for land development

Year	Name of Act	Section
1965	Manchester Corporation	9
1966	Leeds Corporation	6
	Brighton Corporation	4
	Liverpool Corporation (General Powers)	6
1967	Guildford Corporation	4
	Portsmouth Corporation	10
1968	Cheshire County Council	15
	Newcastle-upon-Tyne Corporation	20
	Hounslow Corporation	7
	Durham County Council	8
1969	Bradford Corporation	6
	Kidderminster Corporation	13
	Bedford Corporation	5
	Worcestershire County Council	11
1970	Havering Corporation	3
	Leicestershire County Council	6
	East Suffolk County Council	4
	Somerset County Council	14
	Bootle Corporation	8
	Cumberland County Council	22
	Monmouthshire County Council	11
1971	Teesside Corporation (General Powers)	21
	Buckingham County Council	6
	Torbay Corporation	21
	Surrey County Council	5
	Exeter Corporation	28
	Isle of Wight County Council	16
	Bournemouth Corporation	9
	Scunthorpe Corporation	32
	Oxfordshire County Council	12
1972	Port Talbot	12
	Hampshire County Council	7
	Devon County Council	5
	Coventry Corporation	15
1973	Glamorgan County Council	7
	Rhondda Corporation	13
	Salford Corporation	4

In the present unsettled state of the property market it can be appreciated that there are certainly losses to be made in property development, but it should be appreciated that most property companies are in trouble because they have not arranged adequate long-term financing. . . . the local authority is in fact a better investment risk (for insurance companies and pension funds) than many property companies.[47]

(C) LOCAL AUTHORITY SHAREHOLDING FOR NON-DEVELOPMENT PURPOSES

Many authorities have acquired supplementary powers individually to lend money to firms. Between 1963 and 1973, authorities in non-assisted as well as assisted areas, acquired the necessary legal provisions to provide loans. We have argued earlier that loans to industry were insufficient in the crisis. Local authorities have sought other powers to provide assistance which does not have the disadvantages of loans. In 1976 Tyne and Wear County Council acquired powers permitting it and District Councils in its area to make interest relief and rent relief grants to companies; South Glamorgan County Council acquired powers to help firms with grants to buy secondhand machinery which they could not get from central government. Local authorities have also increasingly tried to acquire powers to subscribe for and acquire shares, advocating that both government regional and industrial policy are insufficient in providing equity assistance for small firms, and pressing for more attention to be given to the problems of small firms in metropolitan areas.

The Director of Economic Planning for Tyne and Wear County Council described the background to his county's proposals as follows:

The encouragement of new firms, and existing but small firms, poses a number of problems. One is that, no matter how attractive the production and sales possibilities, these firms are frequently deficient in mortgagable assets and are constrained by the increased risk of failure which is brought about by excessive fixed interest borrowing. On the other hand, such firms are seldom large enough to apply for public quotation and yet their owners are fiercely independent and therefore unwilling to lose control by merging with a larger company. It is against this background that the County resolved to seek the power to provide equity as well as a flexible system of loan finance.

The private sector provides only a limited financial service to small firms especially when they are newly formed. In part this is because the cost of assessing projects is high in relation to the sums advanced, especially where the firm has little or no track record. However, these abnormally high assessment costs can be justified in the light of the particular economic development problems facing Tyne and Wear, i.e. this is one of the forms which regional subsidy takes. Moreover, local government is particularly well suited to provide a service of this kind. This is because local authorities are self contained units, rooted in the communities they serve and directly responsible to their own electorate. They can therefore make contact with and assist even the very small firms which are scattered throughout their areas. In order to carry out this task they do not need, and do not have, the cumbersome administrative superstructure which would be necessary if a national organisation were to seek such small scale involvement with industry, and yet maintain an unbroken chain of responsibility for the stewardship of public funds. It is extremely doubtful therefore whether central government (or any other nationwide organisation, such as the National Enterprise Board) would be well fitted to provide a really efficient service to new firms, or to small firms even though they have been established for some time.[48]

When the Council was unsuccessful in obtaining legal powers to acquire equity for these purposes it then started to explore other legal possibilities for achieving its objectives, including the use of supplementary provision of existing legislation.

There was further pressure from other authorities in their attempt to respond to a situation in which their legal powers were small. The Greater London Council, for instance, proposed the formation of a comprehensive industrial policy for London which included the examination of the role of London Transport to see whether it could make a contribution towards expanding its industrial base or otherwise assist towards expanding industrial policies.[49] Subsequently, London Transport entered into discussions with British Leyland about enlarging a Leyland truck plant in West London for the production of buses, with the possibility of increased employment in the plant. The consortium was to be backed by the other PTEs.[50] The project would contribute towards employment objectives as well as reducing the costs to PTEs and London Transport of maintaining and repairing their existing unsatisfactory vehicle stock.

By 1976/7 the number of official documents arguing for policy change was increasing. The Standing Conference on London and South-East Regional Planning reported in 1977 that policy changes were needed to tackle the problems of inner London and the national decline in the proportion of small firms.[51] The Strategic Plan for the Northern Region argued for policy changes to ensure greater managerial support and financial assistance for small firms and new enterprises which were under-represented in the Region.[52] The Royal Town Planning Institute pressed for inner city local authorities to regenerate firms and economic activity in their areas, and pointed out the initiative which South Yorkshire County Council had taken in investing its pension fund in small firms in its area.[53] The West Midlands County Council Economic Review in 1977 argued that metropolitan problems were more serious than regional problems: government policy should change and be based on aid to inner cities; a greater proportion of aid should be diverted to benefit small companies; and there should be a concentration on strengthening industries which would help employment in metropolitan areas.[54] In 1977 Merseyside County Council began discussions with the National Enterprise Board to help small locally based enterprises with growth potential; the council would identify which firms needed assistance and the NEB would provide the financial assistance and 'acquire a stake in the companies it helped'.[55] It was argued that 'the plan could help to allay fears in the English regions that the Scottish and Welsh development agencies are proving more flexible than the NEB and better able to create local job opportunities. MPs in areas such as the North-East have been worried that the board is too busy digesting British Leyland to be of much immediate help to them'.[56]

Finally, in the spring of 1977 the Secratary of State for the Environment announced:

> We shall introduce legislation to enhance the powers of local authorities with serious inner area problems to enable them to assist industry and to designate industrial improvement areas. We shall encourage local authorities to give more consideration to the needs of industry, particularly of small firms, in their planning policies.[57]

Local authority shareholding was not amongst the new proposed powers.

These pressures, proposals and policies reflected an increasing identification of local authorities with the needs of small firms, and they also reflected the limitations on implementing proposals. They show to some extent the division of interests between central government and large companies on the one hand, and local government and small companies on the other. Our later analysis will explain how regional authorities fit into this and also what part local authority shareholding for land development plays in this division of interests.

V CONCLUDING REMARKS

Between 1968 and 1975 local and regional authority shareholding began and grew. Figure 2 shows the geographical spread of local and regional authority shareholding. Part II will deal in greater detail with the more specific reasons for this shareholding. It will build on the background provided in this chapter and will be based on the three developments in the crisis we have outlined:

> firstly, the capital restructuring of the economy, the role of big and small firms;
> secondly, the influence or control over property development;
> and thirdly, the reduction of unproductive aspects of state expenditure.

We will see the unique attributes of shareholding as a state instrument

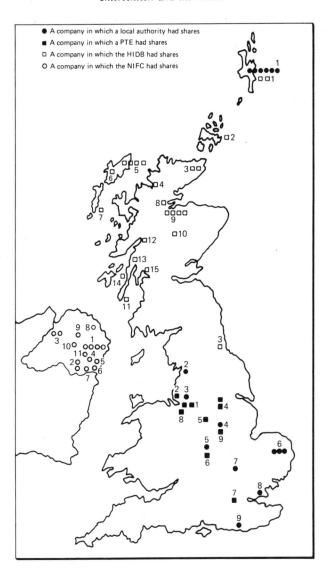

FIGURE 2 Local and regional authority shareholding in the United Kingdom
1968–77

Local authority companies ●
1 Shetland Towage Ltd   Shetland Islands Council
    Grandmet Shetland Ltd

Sullom Voe Association Ltd
Zetland Finance Ltd
Shetland Norse Preserving Ltd
Shetland Aggregates Ltd

2	Blackburn Rovers Football and Athletic Co. Ltd	Blackburn D.C.
3	Manchester Mortgage Corporation Ltd	Manchester D.C.
4	Horizon Midlands Ltd	Nottinghamshire C.C.
5	National Exhibition Centre Ltd	Birmingham D.C.
6	Colegate Developments Ltd	Norwich D.C.
	Colegate Investments Ltd	
	Conesford Developments Ltd	
7	Buckingham Borough Development Co. Ltd	Aylesbury Vale D.C. and Buckinghamshire C.C.
8	Thames Estuary Development Co. Ltd	Southend D.C.
9	Brighton Civic Development Co. Ltd	Brighton D.C.

Passenger Transport Executive companies ■

1	Lancashire United Transport Ltd	Greater Manchester
	SELNEC Transport Services Ltd	
2	Merseyside Passenger Transport Services Ltd	Merseyside
3	Tyneside Transport Services Ltd	Tyne and Wear
4	Hanson Coach Services Ltd	West Yorkshire
	Baddeley Brothers (Holmfirth) Ltd	
5	Booth & Fisher (Sales & Services) Ltd	South Yorkshire
6	Pearson Green Ltd	West Midlands
	West Midlands Passenger Transport Ltd	
7	London Transport International Services Ltd	London Transport
8	National Transport Tokens Ltd	All PTEs
9	Horizon Midlands Ltd	Greater Manchester

Highlands and Islands Development Board companies □

1 Shetland Hotels (Lerwick) Ltd
Shetland-Norse Preserving Co. Ltd
2 J. Anderson (Boatbuilders) Ltd, Stromness, Orkney
3 Caithness Glass Ltd, Wick
4 Thaneway Ltd
5 Clansman Holdings Ltd, Stornoway, Isle of Lewis
Manor Hotel Ltd
Mackenzie Building Supplies Ltd
Jennifreeth Ltd
6 Maricult Flotation Ltd, Uig, Isle of Lewis
7 Highland Trout Co. Ltd, South Uist
8 Hi-Fab Ltd, Muir of Ord, Inverness
9 Jacobite Cruises Ltd, Inverness
Castle Stuart Foods Ltd
North Scottish Helicopters Ltd
Bands of Inverness Ltd

10 Cairngorm Sports Developments Ltd, Aviemore
11 Lennon and Kean Ltd, Campbeltown
12 UEG Trials Ltd, Fort William
13 Scottish Sea Farms Ltd, Oban
14 Gateway West Argyll, Lochgilphead, Argyll
15 Dunoon Ceramics Ltd, Argyll
Northern Ireland Finance Corporation companies 0
  1 Northern Ireland Leather Co. Ltd, Belfast
    Ards Holdings
    Strathearn Audio
    Fonnom Ltd
  2 Andus Electronics Ltd, Craigavan
    Oakland Foods Ltd
  3 Ben Sherman Group, Londonderry
    Regna International Ltd
  4 United Chrometainers Ltd, Killyleagh
  5 John Cleland and Son Ltd, Carryduff
  6 Crawford Textiles Ltd, Dunmurry
  7 Glen Electric Co. Ltd, Newry
  8 Colin J. Brook Ltd, Carrickfergus
  9 G.H. Patents Ltd, Magherafelt
 10 Regal Styles Ltd, Markethill
 11 C. Walker & Sons Ltd, Lisburn
    Princes Development Co. Ltd, Hillsborough

for securing these three objectives. We shall also stress again that each geographical area may have its own unique factors which differentiate it from other areas but that, so far as shareholding is concerned, Shetland, the Highlands, London, the inner city, or any area is not a 'special case'. Local and regional authority shareholding performs a role which relates to the national processes we have discussed.

The next chapter will provide some analysis of the different kinds of state enterprise which have developed since the last century, and amongst which shareholding at the local and regional levels has recently emerged. It will concentrate on the difference between nationalisation/municipalisation on the one hand, and shareholding on the other. This will provide us with a further guide to the specific functions performed by local and regional authority shareholding which we can then develop in Part II.

2 Municipal Socialism or Local Capitalism

The previous chapter examined the recent context of local and regional authority shareholding. This chapter explores the entrepreneurial activities of the state at the local, regional and national levels since the mid-nineteenth century when the introduction of limited liability in companies reduced the risk to shareholders and enabled the massive investment of private capital in manufacturing industry, the growth of large-scale industry and the growth in the number of companies. In particular, the chapter is concerned with the developing role of the state in individual enterprises at the local, regional and national levels during this developing process of capital accumulation. This provides the historical context for examining the mechanisms of local and regional shareholding in further detail.

I STATE ENTERPRISE

The concept of state enterprise has been defined very loosely in the past and must be clarified according to the functions that different kinds of state enterprise can perform in the accumulation process. State enterprise performs certain functions that private capital normally fulfils, and at different periods different forms of state enterprise dominate because they are more appropriate for particular functions. Nationalisation, municipal enterprise or trading, and state shareholding are the three major forms which we examine here. In each case a degree of risk is taken by the state as owner or shareholder which varies according to the function being performed.

By taking or sharing in the risk of a venture the state performs a role as an individual part of capital subject to the law of value in the accumulation process; it may be involved in the direct creation of surplus-value which is appropriated either by the state or by others; or alternatively the state may facilitate the creation of surplus-value. Many activities of the state, other than state enterprise, facilitate the creation of surplus-value, including the provision of council houses and the education of the workforce. Activities other than state enterprise also appropriate surplus-value, for instance company taxation. In none of these does the state act as a risk-taker directly involved as an *individual* part of capital in the accumulation process. Not all private capital is involved in the direct creation of surplus-value; for instance, private investment in property, land, and banks. But all this private capital takes risks to a greater or lesser extent by entering the accumulation process, and like productive capital it grows through takeover and merger.

All capital exchanges commodities, or extracts a return for land or money, on an individual entrepreneurial basis in unrestricted, open markets. As individual parts of total capital all enterprises are affected by the ability of productive labour to create an adequate rate of surplus-value and for that surplus-value to be realised in exchanges of commodities. The state as entrepreneur is subject to the same laws as an individual private entrepreneur.

There is some difference between the state as a capitalist and the private entrepreneur as a capitalist. This is brought about by the fact that the state takes on certain kinds of activity and certain kinds of risk which the private entrepreneur does not. In other words, there *is* a difference between the way the state acts as entrepreneur and the way the private sector acts as entrepreneur. What this difference is will be unravelled in the following chapters.

State entrepreneurial activity as we have described it takes three forms: nationalisation, municipalisation and shareholding. Nationalisation means the ownership, financing and management of an industry or firm by a body appointed by the state, and it can take three forms. The first is 'departmental socialism' in which state departments are themselves involved in the running of businesses taken over by the state.[1] This option was effectively rejected by the Labour Party in the 1920s because of its precarious political position. The public or statutory corporation, the second form of nationalisation, was accepted by the Labour Party as a compromise between departmental socialism and guild socialism in which state takeovers are handed over to workers' guilds.[2] A statutory corporation is a separate state agency formed to run a whole or the main part of an industry taken into public ownership. It is managed by a state-appointed board, for example the National Coal Board, and has strict *ultra vires* (it can only do what it is legally empowered to do); it is created by a special Act of Parliament, and is accountable to Parliament through a Select Committee.[3] The public corporation reconciled two conflicting principles in early Labour Party thinking on the matter. 'It was a device of socialism and a sound business proposition'.[4] This combination of commercial objectives and public control was epitomised in Herbert Morrison's plans for the setting up of the London Passenger Transport Board in 1933. The third form of nationalisation is the chartered corporation whereby a charter of incorporation is granted by the Crown. This has no *ultra vires* and is very difficult for Parliament and the courts to control, and it is rarely used.[5] Today there are eighty statutory or chartered corporations.

Municipalisation or municipal enterprise is defined similarly as the operation of an enterprise by a body appointed by a local authority – usually a local authority department. Unlike the national level of government, the local level has been more involved in 'departmental socialism'. The main examples of municipal enterprise are the production of gas, water and electricity services. Gas and electricity have since been nationalised, or taken over as public corporations at the national level of government. Water provision has been reorganised and concentrated at the regional level. Other municipal enterprise, such as road transport provision, has remained to a large extent at the local level.

State shareholding refers to the ownership of shares in a limited company by national government or by a regional or local authority. Most state shareholding up to the early 1970s has taken place via the nationalised industries, many of which own companies as part of their inheritance on nationalisation or as part of the nationalised industries' normal business operations. Altogether hundreds of private companies are involved in this way.

These different forms of intervention have performed different functions in the historical periods in which each was predominant. This is because of the different ways in which they acted as individual capitals to produce or facilitate the production of surplus-value, and because of the different ways in which the surplus-value was appropriated. Local authority shareholding must be seen in the context of the historical development of municipal enterprise, nationalisation and shareholding at different levels. From the mid-nineteenth century for some ninety years municipal enterprise was the dominant form of state entrepreneurial activity. After its heyday which was ended by the post-Second World War nationalisation of public utilities and essential services, it declined in importance and was not replaced by any other mechanism for economic planning at the local level. The interventionist role of local authorities in industry was reduced to that of indirect influence through physical land-use incentives and controls.

There was no history at all of state enterprise at the regional level. The rise of shareholding at the local and regional levels and the renewed interest in municipal enterprise and other mechanisms for directly intervening in the local economy has occurred at a time when nationalisation has been replaced by shareholding as the major form of new state entrepreneurial activity at the national level. In other words, the same *form* of intervention is now occurring at all levels at the same time. While state enterprise occurs on a large-scale only at the national level, it is growing at the local and regional levels, and the beginnings are evident of an economic planning function existing at all levels for the first time in history.

II THE RISE AND FALL OF MUNICIPAL ENTERPRISE

The earliest examples of municipal enterprise developed in medieval times when municipalities took responsibility variously for the water supply, the conduct of markets, and the management of harbours and docks in order to facilitate the smooth operation of agriculture and fishing. During the nineteenth century municipal enterprise became very widespread, developing in an *ad hoc* way through Local Acts of Parliament, and mainly for the purposes of providing utilities – gas, water, electricity, ports and harbours – and trading services such as transport. These services were essential for the production of manufacturing industry so it is not surprising that local authorities in the North of England pioneered the way. In London progress in obtaining powers was slower because manufacturing industry was less well-developed and because the cost of buying up the large companies involved was high.

This type of municipal enterprise benefited manufacturing industry in a number of ways. The private utility companies concerned were few in number and were rapidly gaining monopoly positions in the economy, increasing the costs to manufacturing industry and reducing the potential size of the surplus-value produced by manufacturing industry which was needed for reinvestment and the growth of industry. In addition, these types of enterprise required high levels of fixed capital expenditure compared with revenue obtainable, resulting in their uneven development between and within authorities. Meanwhile, the commodities they produced were needed by manufacturing industry in a smooth and regular supply. Local authorities had regarded it as their responsibility to take over these activities in order to reduce the high cost of these services to the population and industry in the towns. Gradually, enabling powers were passed empowering certain or all local authorities to provide major services, and by 1936/7 one quarter of all local authority annual expenditure (including rates, grants-in-aid, and the trading services) was accounted for in this way.[6]

While the supply of these services to industry benefited capital as a whole and assisted in the process of capital accumulation, national government did not consider it necessary to intervene in the economy. There was little change in the attitude of national government towards greater intervention in the economy throughout the nineteenth or early twentieth century, despite the change from boom conditions in the 1830s and 1840s to the intermittent crisis conditions of the 1880s to 1930s. During these crises, British industry responded in a limited way to the need to increase productivity and restructure productive capacity, or, rather, to change the conditions of production in order to increase the mass of surplus-value relative to the existing capital. Rather than introduce the technological changes needed, which would have increased productivity and increased the competitive nature of industry within the industrialised nations of the world, the government encouraged an increase in trading activity in new markets abroad.[7] There were only two small changes in central government's attitude during this period. One was the introduction of public works programmes, the other was the introduction of limited nationalisation.

The public works programmes grew out of a response by government at the national level to public protests against unemployment which culminated in 'mob violence'[8] in the Trafalgar Square riot of 1886. Joseph Chamberlain's Local Government Board circular was issued one month later encouraging local authorities to undertake public works (as an alternative to poor relief) to reduce some of the unemployment and for the first time expressed 'the acceptance by the government of the principle that unemployment was a problem of society, not the result of want of virtue, or of laziness in an individual'.[9] The circular was reissued several times after 1886 and led eventually to the Unemployed Workmen Act of 1905. Under this Act, powers were given to local authorities to provide work in labour colonies (as well as to set up Labour Exchanges and to train workers for migration or emigration).

The Act was fought for strenuously by local authorities and by the LCC in particular, and enabled them to provide public works such as the building and running of crematoria, markets, prisons, harbours, local transport services, and the manufacture of armaments. However, these activities were doomed to failure from the start because they were 'external to the normal commercial and industrial system'.[10] The public works programmes represented an attempt by many local authorities to tackle the economic problems of their area by providing employment for the vast unemployed population. But the surplus-value or return on capital obtained in the production process was low because the labour content in the production process was proportionately high, production was not continuous, and there was no market for the commodities produced other than public authorities. This solution to unemployment was a political expedient and did not contribute directly to the process of capital accumulation.

The second area in which central government's approach was modified in this period was in relation to nationalisation. A small number of existing or new industries were nationalised between 1900 and the Second World War. These included the Port of London Authority, the Forestry Commission, the Central Electricity Generating Board (though the electricity industry was not fully nationalised because 'authorised authorities' could still produce and distribute electricity), the Metropolitan Water Board, the BBC, the Racecourse Betting Control Board, the London Passenger Transport Board, and the British Overseas Airways Corporation. However, state intervention in the national economy during this period was gradual, reluctant, limited, and did not at any time constitute part of an overall strategy.

At the local level throughout the nineteenth century and early twentieth century, the municipalisation of gas, water and electricity was evolutionary in nature, but much more systematic than national government's promotion of public works programmes or public ownership activities. General enabling powers for the public supply of these services by local authorities were granted sometimes after long periods of public outcry against the high charges for them. For instance, the Public Health Act of 1848 empowered the transfer of privately owned waterworks to town councils but general enabling provisions for the public supply of gas did not occur until 1875, and for electricity in 1882 (through licences or compulsory purchase after twenty-one years and with other limitations). Often these undertakings were profitable in the early years after takeover, but increasingly they became more heavily 'subsidised' out of the rates.

Municipal enterprise took risks and was often directly involved in the creation of surplus-value, but its pricing policy was not set in relation to the heavy capital expenditure involved, for instance, in reservoirs, water mains, gas and electricity generating plant and networks of pipes and cables. In other words, prices were set at a level which did not cover the cost-price of production. Not only was any surplus-value produced by the municipal enterprises being appropriated by private enterprise, but often the failure of the enterprises to cover the costs of production made them unprofitable or loss-making in financial terms. By paying for commodities produced by municipal enterprise at less than their cost of production, manufacturing industry was able to increase its profitability, lower the prices of its commodities, and increase its competitiveness. By 1937 £2,525,970[11] was transferred from the rates to make up deficiences in the various municipal undertakings about half of which went to subsidise water undertakings. Also, the loan debt for these undertakings incurred by local authorities was extremely high, in 1937 amounting to £484,495,545.[12] Where gas, water and electricity undertakings remained in private hands attempts were also made to lower the costs of the services produced. For instance, there were often legally circumscribed restrictions on the level of dividends that a company could pay, and requirements that any surplus beyond prescribed limits was to be applied to the reduction of charges and not be made available to the shareholders.

During the nineteenth and early twentieth centuries many other examples of what are commonly understood to be municipal enterprise arose. For instance, local authorities were empowered to undertake, under General Acts, Orders under General Acts, or under Local Private Acts, such things as the running of markets for the retail of fish, fruit, vegetables, poultry, livestock, etc., civic restaurants, crematoria, baths and wash-houses, and racecourses. A few of these remain today, for instance the well-known Hull telephone service, Birmingham Municipal Bank, the Bradford Conditioning House and various racecourses. Since the Second World War new municipal enterprises have been confined generally to the fields of leisure or culture, for instance sports centres, theatres and festivals. Some of these examples were unique to a single local authority; others were introduced into a number of authorities. Only a few of them such as civic restaurants, the Birmingham Bank, the telephone service and the Conditioning House, involve the local authority in risk taking. None were introduced at the local level on the same scale as the utilities.

There are three types of municipal enterprise which grew up in the nineteenth century and which have survived on a substantial scale today at the local and regional levels. These are water provision, transportation, and public works or direct labour organisations.

Water provision remained the responsibility of local authorities and joint boards of local authorities until it was transferred to Regional Water Authorities under the 1973 Water Act. The exception to this was the Metropolitan Water Board which was nationalised in the 1920s. In 1976 proposals were put forward to nationalise the whole water industry.[13] These included the establishment of a National Water Authority with stronger central powers than the existing National Water Council, and a consequent reduction in the powers of the Regional Water Authorities. The proposals also included taking over twenty-eight private water companies which still existed and which accounted for 22 per cent of the water supply and 19 per cent of the area of England and Wales. The Companies' profits and dividends were controlled by statute, just like the old private gas and electricity companies of the nineteenth and early twentieth century.

Transport also remained the responsibility of local authorities and some private undertakings. In 1968, as we mentioned in the Introduction, the National Bus 'Company' (NBC) was set up to control road passenger services on a regional basis in England and Wales. It also engaged in bus manufacture jointly with British Leyland. The 1968 Transport Act established three conurbation passenger transport authorities, in Merseyside, West Midlands and South-East Lancashire/North-East Cheshire (SELNEC). The London Transport Executive was set up in 1969 under the GLC as a much-altered descendent of the Herbert Morrison public corporation, the London Passenger Transport Board. In 1974 three more passenger transport authorities and executives were established under the control of the new metropolitan counties, West Yorkshire, South Yorkshire and Tyne and Wear, and in 1975 the Greater Glasgow PTE was established. The boundaries of the original PTEs were changed as well to coincide with the new metropolitan county areas and SELNEC PTE was renamed Greater Manchester PTE. At this time there were still many private stage carriage, coach and bus travel companies in existence which were either taken over or came to operating agreements with the NBC or the PTEs.

In addition to road transport, local authorities owned thirty-two aerodromes in 1966, a number of them operated by consortia of local authorities, such as East Midlands Airport (Derby, Derbyshire, Nottingham, Nottinghamshire, Leicestershire). The largest local authority airport, in terms of business, was at Manchester.

There were also a number of local authority-owned ports and harbours. Some were converted for entertainment and recreation but many, including the largest at Bristol, were primarily concerned with trading. Although not a municipally-owned port, the Port of Manchester was ultimately controlled by Manchester Corporation through the major interest of the Council in the Manchester Ship Canal Company which owned and operated the port.

Like water and passenger transport there were aspects of ports and harbours which were nationalised or for which there were proposals for nationalisation. In 1962 a National Ports Council was set up to assist central planning, and in 1969 proposals were made to establish a more powerful National Ports Authority which would take over a number of ports, including Bristol and Manchester.[14] The proposals were not implemented because of the change in national government in 1970. It was not surprising to find that local authority shareholding occurred in connection with various local transport activities when the recent crisis began to affect their functioning and performance.

The third type of municipal enterprise which has survived on some scale today is the public works department or Direct Labour Organisation (DLO). While the functions of water provision and transportation as state enterprise have remained the same, the function of DLOs has changed. In different periods they have performed different roles in relation to capital as a whole.

Many local authorities run DLOs, the largest being in Manchester, set up in 1967 and employing over 3000 building and other workers. They were not set up to give work to the unemployed, as were the earlier public works programmes, but were intended to provide a reliable service to the local authority, particularly for public house building. John Tilley argues that there has been little political support for the further development of DLOs because,

> the industry . . . falls awkwardly between the three categories of manufacturing industry, public utilities, and service industries. It has aspects of all three, but the 'broad brush' approach which Labour's policymakers tend to adopt for each of the categories is demonstrably inappropriate for the building industry. For example, as manufacturing industry, it undoubtedly has a definite end-product, but increased production cannot help the export drive . . . and in any case the product is usually only manufactured after the customer has been found.[15]

DLOs are unlikely to be expanded or increase in number because of the role they play in relation to capital. Like other examples of municipal enterprise, the DLO is operated entirely within and by the local authority, and its products are sold to the local authority. There is a tendency for the DLOs to be 'inefficiently' run because they have incurred high costs, especially for labour which has not been laid off during recessions in building activity, unlike labour in the private construction industry. This inefficiency has led to the creation of a low rate of surplus-value.

Besides direct labour organisations, local authorities have pressed for other municipal enterprise but so far they have been unsuccessful. The West Midlands County Council, for example, in its Bill of 1975, included provisions for the local authority to manufacture commodities for sale particularly in the local area, such as house furniture, school furniture, school clothing, bricks, timber and joinery materials.[16] The aim had been mainly to manufacture commodities not otherwise produced locally. Opposition to the Bill centred on the impossibility of a local authority competing fairly with local industry which, it was claimed, might be producing similar commodities now or in the future.

Throughout its history, municipal enterprise has been affected by political opinion. It was consistently supported by socialists such as the Fabians and the Progressive Movement at the turn of the century, who claimed that municipal enterprise was a forerunner to the public ownership of all industry and of a socialist society. Its opponents claimed that it would interfere with local competition amongst private firms because local authorities can obtain loans more easily and cheaply than the private sector, particularly at times when credit is scarce or expensive, and would undermine the incentive for private firms to trade. Other arguments are that it too easily incurs 'losses' to the local authority, that it is time-consuming for Councillors and officers, that the government should not become heavily involved in labour questions, that some types of municipal enterprise, for example DLOs, strengthen trade unions and so push up wage rates, that the trade unions should not be allowed to influence public sector wages, and that it leads to unfair pricing policies.

Both the socialist arguments in favour, and the variety of arguments against, are ideological in nature and do not consider the function of municipal enterprise in different historical periods. In its heyday, municipal enterprise was used to reduce the costs to private manufacturing industry in the ways we have described earlier. There was nothing 'socialist' about it; instead it was the state functioning as capital, performing a special function for the benefit of capital as a whole by supplying commodities to private industry below their value and often below their cost. Acceptance by some local authorities of the more systematic use of municipal enterprise again today implies a re-establishment of the need for state enterprise at the local level. State enterprise at this level had declined since the Second World War and these demands for its reinstatement reflect a general shift towards a greater involvement by the local level of the state in the local economy. But, as we shall demonstrate, municipalisation is not the most appropriate form of state enterprise during the present period for benefiting capital as a whole.

III THE NATIONALISATION OF LOCAL ECONOMIC FUNCTIONS

Nationalisation was introduced in different periods throughout the twentieth century for military, defence and national economic reasons where it was considered that particular industries would be most efficiently organised by a central body. After the Second World War a programme of nationalisation was devised by a Labour Government. It included the transfer of most undertakings previously run as municipal enterprise to national agencies, and the creation of state enterprises to run completely new activities. The increase in state enterprise at the national level was part of a more systematic attempt at national economic planning which has survived in various ways ever since, and until recently it performed the same function as municipal enterprise.[17] We briefly examine the history of state enterprise at the national level in so far as it affects and helps to explain the rise of local and regional shareholding.

The major nationalisations occurred between 1946 and 1954 and during this period the types of industry involved were utilities and essential services, and a large number of other individual activities. They began with the Bank of England, the National Coal Board, the Arts Council and the Civil Aviation Authority in 1946; these were followed in 1947 by the nationalisation of the railways and canals, inland waterways, and by the nationalisation of electricity distribution; then in 1948 gas provision was nationalised, and in 1949 the iron and steel industry (named companies only); in 1951 the Whitefish Authority was created and in 1954 the Atomic Energy Authority and the Independent Television Authority.

Much has been written on nationalisation and it has been described as an operating tool of central government and therefore incapable of achieving the 'commercial' objectives of the industries. It is argued that the industries were supposed to be a means of creating a publicly owned monopoly. This monopoly would be separate from government and therefore able to achieve a higher degree of 'freedom, boldness and enterprise in the management of undertakings of an industrial or commercial character' and to 'escape from the caution and circumspection which is considered typical of government departments'.[18] It is assumed that the freedom associated with this model of the nationalised industry prevents it from achieving 'social' objectives. As a result the government must intervene in the industry's operations in order to achieve these objectives.

The debates about nationalisation have been mostly concerned with aspects of public administration, and particularly with the accountability of nationalised industries. It is argued that the ambiguous position of the public corporations, supposedly autonomous but subject to government interference, has forced them to try to achieve both social and commercial objectives which often conflict. The debates are both confused and sterile because they do not examine the primary reason for the existence and function of nationalised industries. Like municipalisation their main function was primarily to provide low-cost material inputs for the production of manufactured commodities, and therefore the necessary regulation of their policies by government was bound to undermine the public corporation form of nationalisation as a quasi-autonomous organisation. While the *form* of the public corporation does undoubtedly create problems of organisation, management and accountability, these are of secondary importance when compared to its function. Indeed, the function can change over time with different degrees of ease, while the form remains the same. The changes in function depend on the needs of capital.

A change of attitude towards nationalised industries developed towards the end of the 1960s when it became apparent that so-called 'demand management' policies were not smoothing out the periods of crisis in economic development, and that unproductive state expenditure might be contributing to the crisis. By 1972–3 'subsidies' to the nationalised industries arising from public sector price restraint were between £4–500m. (with an additional £1,300m. for research and development grants, free depreciation, investment allowances, and employment premia).[19] A policy of eliminating state 'subsidies' was introduced in the Budget of November 1974. The Chancellor announced that the existing subsidy was to be turned into a surplus. This was later shown to mean that the nationalised industries should attempt at least to 'cover costs' and reduce the public corporation deficit in 1975/6 from £550m. to £70m. This was to be effected by a change in pricing policy which in turn would have the effect of decreasing the real wages of consumers and thereby reducing the value of the labour input into the production process in industry as a whole, and increasing the rate of surplus-value created. A second policy was also introduced at that time which was to increase the level of investment in the nationalised industries in order to raise productivity, again having the effect of raising the rate of surplus-value.

These new policies and the recent nationalisation must be seen in relation to the current crisis. The nationalisation of the shipbuilding and aerospace industries in 1977 occurred because substantial government assistance had been given to different firms and projects in those industries for a number of years but without the firms achieving subsequent long-term viability. The industries were considered to be essential to the national economy but could not be made viable through state shareholding in a few of the firms. The nationalisation form was therefore considered appropriate for reorganising and planning these industries. Nevertheless, like other nationalised industries and the companies in which the NEB owns shares, they do not function to 'subsidise' the private sector with cheap commodities. The shipbuilding and aerospace industries, for instance, will be subject to substantial reorganisation and rationalisation by the new public corporations in order to make them viable. Furthermore, like British Steel and British Airways, British Shipbuilders is attempting to get public dividend capital (the new equivalent of equity capital in the private sector) included in its financial structure in order to 'have a chance of proving itself as a viable corporation, and not a permanent lossmaker'.[20] Similar discussions are taking place between British Aerospace and the Treasury.[21]

IV STATE SHAREHOLDING AT THE NATIONAL LEVEL

Government shareholding is being used in a systematic way during the present period but it is not a new form of intervention. In fact state shareholding in limited liability companies registered under the Companies Acts was the first form of state enterprise at the national level. In 1876 the government acquired share capital in the Suez Canal Company in order to assist in the construction of the canal and thereby to encourage trading activity. The company was used again after the Suez crisis of the 1950s in order to settle various compensation claims against Britain. Early this century the government acquired a 25 per cent shareholding in the Cunard Steamship Company in order to prevent foreign firms from acquiring shares, and in 1914 acquired shares in Anglo-Iranian Oil (now BP) in order to ensure necessary oil supplies to the Royal Navy. During the Second World War the government made some minor acquisitions to ensure the production of other military supplies. These and other similar shareholdings were essentially pragmatic, *ad hoc* and arose to solve immediate economic and defence problems. After the Second World War there were occasional attempts to assist particular sectors. Special bodies were set up with powers to provide equity support for firms. These included the National Research Development Corporation which provided support for new technological developments, and a few bodies such as the White Fish Authority, the Herring Industry Board and the National Film Finance Corporation. These bodies and their powers to acquire equity were not part of any national economic planning strategy but were aimed at the solution of particular sectoral problems and the problems of funding new inventions and technology.

Since the mid-1960s state shareholding has been used more systematically. It has taken over from nationalisation as the predominant form of state enterprise wherever this is practicable, because it is more suited than nationalisation to the requirements of industrial restructuring. The IRC was set up in 1966 by a Labour Government, introducing the principle of discrimination and selective intervention in industry, and included amongst its powers the ability to acquire and provide equity for mergers, new investment and reorganisation. This ended the attitude of neutrality towards planning and industry which had characterised the generalised and undiscriminating policy tool of indicative planning of the 1950s and early 1960s. Financial inducements from the IRC that discriminated between firms were to be a positive force by means of which each firm's freedom of action would be widened because the provision of finance, almost always unavailable from other banking sources, enabled the company to pursue lines of action not otherwise open to it.[22] The IRC also found that the firm's new 'freedom of action' had to be guided if maximum use was to be made of public funds. Monitoring procedures had to be developed because the funds were involved in an ongoing situation. This arose particularly where there was a minority shareholding rather than where the company was wholly owned by the state. As a result increasing discriminatory intervention led the government into the whole area of the internal management of the company, while at the same time the prime responsibility for the affairs of the company remained with the board of directors.[23]

The Conservative Government which took power in 1970 abolished the IRC but passed the Industry Act of 1972 which provided for the government to take shareholdings in firms for a variety of purposes. Under this Act shares were acquired in firms by the Department of Trade and Industry. Some of these and other shareholdings were transferred to the NEB in 1975. The NEB was a holding company which was intended to act as a 'catalyst for industrial reorganisation . . . [and also to] manage the government's holdings of shares in firms acquired as part of a more general policy to provide risk in the longer term'.[24] The state used its shareholding powers invested in the NEB for restructuring purposes, investing in profitable firms such as Francis Shaw (rubber and plastics), Computer Analysts and Programmers, and United Medical Company International. (See Table 2.1).

The shareholdings acquired by the NEB rarely involve the state in complete ownership of a company because, as Thornhill states,

> whatever may have been thought to be the virtues of the public corporation 30 years ago, when there was a lot of high-minded talk about combining public responsibility with commercial freedom, events have shown these bodies to be little more than the operating tools of the government. . . . Full and complete ownership of an enterprise has been seen as unnecessary for at least the last decade. The combination of a sizeable shareholding with the government's ordinary regulatory powers over monopolies, prices and fair trading, labour relations and joint stock company management provide as effective a government control, and probably a more flexible one, than complete ownership and

TABLE 2.1 National government shareholding, April 1977 (in percentages)

Department of Industry shareholdings	Government holding as a percentage of total issued ordinary share capital	Other Department shareholding	
*Appledore Shipbuilders Ltd	100	British Petroleum Co. Ltd	48·6
Beagle Aircraft Ltd (in liquidation)		Suez Finance Co. Ltd	7·76
Cable and Wireless Ltd	100	British Sugar Corp. Ltd	11·25
*Cammell Laird Shipbuilders Ltd	50	Power Jets (R&D) Ltd (in liquidation)	100
*Govan Shipbuilders Ltd	100	Toplis & Harding	98·8
John Hastie & Co. Ltd (in receivership)	33·5	Harland & Woolf	100
John Hastie of Greenock (Holdings) Ltd	47		
Kearney & Trekker Marwin Ltd	26		
KTM Machine Tools (Holdings) Ltd	50		
*Marathon Shipbuildings (UK) Ltd	52·3		
*North East Coast Ship-repairers Ltd	100		
Norton Villiers Triumph Ltd	46·4		
SB (Realisations) Ltd	100		
*Sunderland Shipbuilding and Engineering Ltd	100		
*Upper Clyde Shipbuilders Ltd (in liquidation)	48·4		
Wolverhampton Industrial Engines Ltd	100		

*To be incorporated in British Shipbuilders.

TABLE 2.1 (*continued*)

National Enterprise Board Shareholdings

	Government holding as a percentage of total issued ordinary share capital
British Leyland Ltd	95·1
Data Recording Instruments Ltd	53·9
Ferranti Ltd	62·5
Herbert Ltd	100
Rolls Royce (1971) Ltd	100
Agemaspark Ltd	30
Anglo-Venezuelan Railway Corp. Ltd	35
Brown Bovei Kent Ltd	17·6
Cambridge Instrument Ltd	46·3
Dwiford & Elliott Ltd	2·6
International Computer Holdings Ltd	24·4
Twinlock	33·3
Francis Shaw & Co. Ltd	29·8
Computer Analysts & Programmers Ltd	29·9
British Tanners Products Ltd	50
Thwaites & Reed Ltd	90
United Medical Co. International	55
R.R. Chapman (Sub-Sea Surveys) Ltd	45
Pakmet Ltd	34·4
Mollant Engineering Co. Ltd	71
Keland Electrics Ltd	100
Read & Smith Holdings Ltd	29·8
Sinclair Radionics	42·9

management by a public corporation.[25]

State shareholding has a number of advantages as a *form* of intervention. While the form of state enterprise does not, as we have said, determine its function, nevertheless it can make it easier for the state enterprise to operate in a particular way. In particular, the various rules and regulations applying to all companies under the Companies Acts remain the same if the company is wholly or partly owned by the government (or by statutory public corporations). Like the chartered corporation and unlike the statutory corporation, the state may acquire shares in companies without reference to Parliament. Although registered companies are subject to *ultra vires*, the Memorandum of Association is drawn up by the company's promoters and not by Parliament. The clauses which describe the company's 'objects' are usually left as broad as possible and can be altered without reference to Parliament by three-quarters of the shareholders.[26]

Reference to Parliament in the form of legislation *is* needed, however, where, according to a Treasury ruling, 'disbursement of Exchequer funds on a large-scale' is required (about £¾m.–£1m.). Legislation is also needed where assistance is given to a private undertaking whose existence or survival is of importance to the 'national interest'. In both these cases Parliament could have an opportunity to restrict the alterations which may be made to a company's memorandum and articles of association, but the opportunity has never been taken.[27] In addition, the NEB has not so far sought Parliamentary approval for the investment of large capital sums. 'Parliament's prior control of the NEB's operations is limited to approval of the estimates which provide for advances of public dividend capital'.[28]

Apart from these aspects of flexibility which, it is argued, state shareholding provides, there are other factors which are supposed to have prompted its use. Firstly, it is far cheaper than nationalisation or municipalisation. The willingness of the state to back companies with risk capital provides confidence for private capital investment. This may be on a much larger scale than the state's investment. Secondly, it preserves the form of private enterprise. Preservation of the private company form means it is possible to sell the state's shares once the original reason for intervention has gone and, in the case of BP in 1977,[29] £500m. of the state's shares were sold in order to reduce the state's borrowing requirement for other purposes. This makes the mechanism more acceptable than other methods to governments when control or influence over a private firm is needed, either to restructure it or to avoid the social and economic implications of the collapse of particular enterprises.[30] The reselling of shares was a particular feature of Labour's IRC in 1966 and also of the Conservatives' 1972 Industry Act.

Municipal enterprise was followed by nationalisation and then by national shareholding. While there was some overlap these forms of state enterprise occurred during particular historical periods and reflected the different functions that state enterprise plays in the economy. Now local and regional state shareholding has occurred in parallel with the same trends at the national level. This has been brought about by the key elements of the crisis. Centralised economic planning is institutionalised in the NEB. Local and regional shareholding, however, represents a demand for greater sensitivity to local employment and development problems and the problems of small firms. As we shall see, there is nothing 'socialist' about it.

We shall now look in more detail at the ways in which local and regional shareholding has performed its specific functions in the present crisis.

Part II

Local and Regional
Shareholding 1968–77

3 Categorisation of Schemes

In Chapter 1 we outlined three elements of the crisis which have influenced the emergence of local and regional authority shareholding. These were:

(a) the restructuring of British industry, involving an overall reduction of output and productive capital and a conflict between large and small firms;

(b) the need to control or influence a haphazard property market arising out of the increase in speculative office construction;

(c) pressures to reduce state expenditure in so far as it represented a further unproductive charge on surplus-value.

Chapter 2 went on to describe the historical role of state enterprise, particularly at the local level. We discussed how, since 1966, state shareholding has had a particular role to play in restructuring and we referred to arguments about its flexibility, lack of accountability, political appeal, limited state involvement in enterprises and so on. We will now proceed to analyse the specific role that state shareholding plays at the local and regional levels.

I THE TWO BASIC CATEGORIES

Local and regional authorities have become increasingly involved with the economy in their areas. They have intervened in response to the crisis in both property development and in the process of industrial restructuring. Shareholding in these two categories has not been equally represented at the local and regional levels. At the regional level intervention has occurred mainly in manufacturing industry, concerned with, for instance, the production of glassware, textiles, technical equipment or foodstuffs, or commercial ventures of a more general nature involved in the sale of travel tours, in catering and hotelling, or in the operation of helicopters. Shareholding rather than nationalisation/municipalisation was used because the role of state intervention in the crisis was to a large extent 'pump-priming'. The budgets of the regional authorities were not affected by public expenditure restriction but nevertheless were carefully controlled and limited. At the local level intervention has mainly been in land development and infrastructure provision. The property boom ended in the near collapse of the property market as well as leading to the construction of a surplus of office space. The need to encourage building in a controlled way was recognised; shareholding enabled this because it provided a share in the risk and the control of the development, as well as securing a 'return for the community'. The public expenditure cuts affected local authorities directly by making it difficult for them to build, or provide infrastructure for development, as they had done previously; shareholding provided a mechanism for them to do this. The controls introduced by authorities could influence the nature of *the development itself* in accordance with local authority objectives, and they could control any detrimental impact of the development, on *the local economic structure* as well. Shareholding therefore *facilitated* development and infrastructure provision in a controlled way, and overcame problems of cuts and problems of property market instability.

II MANUFACTURE AND COMMERCE: THE LOCAL BACKGROUND

The HIDB was the first public statutory body to be established as a part of regional development policy. It was set up in 1965 to 'assist the people of the Highlands and Islands in their economic and social development and to enable the Highlands and Islands to play a more effective part in the economy and social development of the nation'. The Act of 1965 enabled the Board to give grants and loans to any industrial, commercial or other undertaking, or any activity which in the opinion of the Board would contribute to the economic and social development of the Highlands and Islands. In 1968 the Board gained the power to acquire equity in companies. It subsequently gave loan, grant or equity support in a variety of types of business although it did not concern itself with wholesale and retail distribution, transport and vehicles, or service industries. With a limited budget the Board argued that it should concentrate aid in industries such as manufacturing, processing, tourism, agriculture and fishing on the grounds that service industry would tend to locate where these were established. The HIDB also has a social fund for 'non-economic' projects like village halls, festivals and such-like projects which show no sign of commercial independence.

Table 3.1 shows the percentage of equity held in 23 companies between 1968–76. All are minority shareholdings; 8 represent 30 per cent or more of the total issued share capital and 16 represent 20 per cent of the share capital. In 1976 the Board considered forming a wholly-owned company, but this was exceptional and would have been complementary to its major objectives. The shares were acquired (on negotiation with the firm and with their agreement) often as part of a package of grants, loans and equity, and ususally were accompanied by a capital restructuring on the advice of the Board. The amounts and proportion of grants and loans were

TABLE 3.1 Local and regional authority shareholding in manufacture and commerce

Regional authority	Name of company, % and date of shareholding (financial year ending)	Objects of company and local or regional authority interest
Highlands and Islands Development Board (1968–76)		To acquire equity in companies carrying on or proposing businesses and contributing to the economic or social development of the Highlands and Islands
	Bands of Inverness Ltd, 8%, 1972	Game processing
	Cairngorm Sports Developments Ltd, 39.9%, 1974	Winter sports development
	Caithness Glass Ltd, 34%, 1970	Glass making
	Castle Stuart Foods Ltd, 25%, 1976	Milk products
	Clansman Holdings Ltd, 39%, 1972	Textile manufacture
	Dunoon Ceramics Ltd, n/a, 1975	Ceramics manufacture
	Gateway West Argyll Ltd, 9%, 1971	Fish farming
	Hi-Fab Ltd, 40%, 1972	General engineering
	Highland Trout Ltd, 11%, 1976	Fish farming
	Jacobite Cruises Ltd, 35%, 1976	Holiday cruises
	J. Anderson Ltd, 31%, 1973	Boat building
	Jennifreeth Ltd, 36%, 1973	Garment manufacture
	Lennon & Kean Ltd, 16%, 1970	Optical equipment manufacture
	Mackenzie Building Supplies Ltd, 25%, 1976	Building supplies manufacture
	Manor Hotel Ltd, 21·7%, 1971	Hotel and catering
	Maricult Flotation, 22%, 1976	Fish farming
	North Scottish Helicopters Ltd, 20%, 1973	Helicopter operation
	Scottish Instruments Ltd, 25%, 1973	Mechanical engineering
	Scottish Sea Farms Ltd, 25%, 1970	Fish farming

60

Table 3.1 (*continued*)

Regional authority	Name of company, % and date of shareholding (financial year ending)	Objects of company and local or regional authority interest
	Shetland Hotels Ltd, 23%, 1969	Hotel and retailing
	Shetland-Norse Ltd, 16%, 1976	Fish processing
	Thaneway Ltd, 15%, 1976	Fish farming
	UEG Trials Ltd, 36%, 1975	Underwater equipment development
Northern Ireland Finance Corporation (1972–6)		To acquire equity in order to assist and promote the growth of firms and sectors
	Andus Electronics (UK) Ltd, 40%, 1975	Printed circuit manufacture
	Ards Holdings Ltd, 28%, 1974	Building
	Ben Sherman Group, 100%, 1973	Shirt manufacture
	Colin J. Brook & Co. Ltd, 33·3%, 1973	Precision engineering
	Crawford Textiles Ltd, 40%, 1974	Textile manufacture
	C. Walker & Sons Ltd, 49·9%, 1974	Steel stock holding
	Fonnom Ltd, 100%, 1975	Holding for Sherman Assets
	G. H. Patents Ltd, 100%, 1973	Bus equipment manufacture
	Glen Electric Co. Ltd, 66·6%, 1974	Heater manufacture
	John Cleland & Sons Ltd, 25%, 1975	Printing and carton manufacture
	Northern Ireland Leather Co. Ltd, 100%, 1974	Leather production
	Oakland Foods Ltd, 80·4%, 1974	Food manufacture
	Princes Development Co. Ltd, 75%, 1974	Insulated pipes manufacture
	Regal Styles Ltd, 30·5%, 1973	Garment manufacture
	Regna International Ltd, 100%, 1974	Cash register manufacture
	Strathearn Audio Ltd, 100%, 1974	Audio equipment manufacture
	United Chrometanners Ltd, 44·8%, 1973	Leather tanning

Local authority	Name of company, % and date of shareholding (financial year ending)	Objects of company and local or regional authority interest
Nottinghamshire C.C.	Horizon Midlands Ltd, 10%, 1975	To protect the financial interest of the Council in the management of the East Midlands Airport by supporting a holiday tour company
Shetland Islands Council	Shetland-Norse Preserving Ltd, 32%, 1976	To help a fish processing firm in need of equity capital, as part of Council policy to maintain a viable local economy with long-term growth potential for when North Sea oil is worked out
	Shetland Aggregates Ltd, 51%, 1977	To form a joint co. to excavate and supply aggregates
	Zetland Finance Co. Ltd, 100%, 1974	To raise money for the Council and the local economy
Blackburn D.C.	Blackburn Rovers Football and Athletic Co. Ltd, insignificant %, 1974	To provide financial support to a football club, in order to promote the sale of shares in the club so that the existence of the club helps promote the area for investment purposes
Local authority PTEs		
West Yorkshire PTE	Hanson Coach Services Ltd, Baddeley Brothers (Holmfirth) Ltd; both wholly owned, 1974 and 1976	To provide a substantial base for coaching operations and expansion into leisure travel
South Yorkshire PTE	Booth & Fisher (Sales and Services) Ltd, wholly owned, 1975	Part of bus and coach firm integrated into PTE: operates petrol sales and car repairs

TABLE 3.1 (*continued*)

Local authority PTEs	Name of company, % and date of shareholding (financial year ending)	Objects of company and local or retional authority interest
Greater Manchester PTE	Horizon Midlands Ltd, 14%, 1975–6 (10% through a PTE subsidiary)	To expand PTE tour interests
London Transport Executive	London Transport International Services Ltd, wholly owned, 1976	To provide profitable consultancy services on aspects of transport engineering
Local authority proposals		
South Yorkshire Metropolitan C.C.	1976: To invest proportion of county pension fund in local industry	
GLC/London Transport	1977: To form company to manufacture buses in partnership with British Leyland	

dependent on the individual circumstances of the firm and the scale of the proposed development.

The types of firm supported by the HIDB have been varied but the majority are industries which use the natural resources of the Highlands, such as fishing, tourism, game processing, and cheese making, or else are traditional to the Highlands, such as weaving. In two cases craft industries were supported because they were considered suitable to rural areas even though they had been 'artificially' introduced. Other industries supported have been those which require a high level of technology and which are not traditional to any area of the country, such as the manufacture of optical equipment and the operation of helicopters, or industries which supply commodities for local consumption, such as boats and engineering.

In the majority of cases the HIDB has supported firms either from the outset or after two or three years when they have reached a critical growth point and require financial assistance and capital restructuring. However, there are important exceptions such as Clansman Holdings and Caithness Glass. The HIDB gave assistance to these firms after they had operated for many years, become important employers in their areas, and reached a point where a large capital input was needed in order to grow or restructure.

The NIFC was the second public statutory body to be established as part of regional development policy. In 1971 the Cairncross Committee was set up to review the economic and social development of Northern Ireland. The Committee reported back the same year with recommendations that a special institution be set up to provide substantial financial resources to the private sector of industry. As a result, the Northern Ireland Finance Corporation was set up under the Northern Ireland Finance Corporation (N.I.) Order 1972. It was initially set up for three years, though its life was extended until it was replaced by the Northern Ireland Development Agency in 1976.

The fundamental objective of the NIFC was to 'assist the economy of Northern Ireland by:

(a) preserving the essential fabric of industry and commerce;
(b) helping to establish an improved industrial structure upon which a sounder economy could be developed'.

From the outset the NIFC had power to provide financial assistance in the form of equity. The specific objectives of the NIFC depended on its ability to affect the capital structure of a firm and to exercise some continuous control over the financial and management affairs of a firm. These specific objectives included the maintenance and improvement of the following:

- the profitability and efficiency of industry;
- employment levels, notably in growth industries;

- the methods and amount of investment in Northern Ireland industry and its competitiveness in the UK, the Republic of Ireland and world markets;
- the quality of Northern Ireland management;
- the indigenous share of ownership and control of companies, designs and patents, etc.;
- research and development of new products, technologies, and business methods.

To achieve these objectives the NIFC functioned both at the level of an individual firm and within an industry as a whole. Assistance was limited to manufacturing industry or certain service industries which were closely associated with manufacturing. It operated as a separate body but in cooperation with the Department of Commerce, which had a broad range of powers to assist industry including the provision for giving grants for factories and other purposes.

Table 3.1 shows the percentage equity holdings of the NIFC in 17 companies between 1972 and 1976. The percentages range from 28 per cent to 100 per cent. They are generally larger than HIDB holdings in firms because there were greater restrictions on the proportions of share capital that the HIDB could acquire without the approval of the Secretary of State for the region. Like the HIDB, the NIFC/NIDA concentrated on assisting manufacturing industry but the size of firm was generally larger and the type of firm more varied. They were willing to give assistance wherever there was a chance of creating profitability, and particularly where the basis existed for the development of a whole industry. Some firms are based on the area's natural resources, like beef manufacture (9·3 per cent of the Northern Ireland labour force work in agriculture compared to 2·4 per cent for Great Britain), but examples of other industries supported are more numerous, amongst them the manufacture of textiles, furniture and precision instruments.

At the local authority level the local circumstances leading to shareholding in manufacturing and commerce were very varied. In no authority so far have interventions of this type been as systematic as they were at the regional level. They have been confined to single ventures except in Shetland, where the council acquired shares in three companies, but this was because the authority had greater legal powers for this category of shareholding than any other authority.

Oil was discovered in the North Sea off the coast of Scotland in 1969/70. A cluster of oilfields was located within the East Shetland Basin of the North Sea, the main fields being Ninian and Brent. Most of the oil was to be brought ashore on the Shetland Islands. The Shetland Islands Council (SIC) was very concerned that Shetland should preserve its own industry despite oil, since the oil developments were going to be relatively short-lived. After that the islands would have to rely on their own economic structure in order to survive. In the meantime there would be considerable strain imposed on the economic and social structure of Shetland. The council's Research and Development Department monitored traditional industries on the assumption that Shetland must continue to produce commodities itself in the short and long term. It would be helped by a 'disturbance allowance' which the Council was obtaining from the oil revenues of the oil companies and by legal powers contained in the 1974 Zetland County Council Act.

One firm in which the SIC acquired shares was Shetland-Norse Limited. The collapse of this firm threatened employment in a relatively remote area of the islands. The company had experienced heavy losses due to slumps in the supply of crab and then in the supply of white fish, but it had the prospect of substantial growth with a contract from John West Ltd for tinned crab. It faced a short-term liquidity problem because of its difficulty as a Norwegian firm in raising further British finance with its variable record. The Highlands and Islands Development Board was already involved with the firm, but there were limits on the extent to which the HIDB could act alone. The HIDB regarded the firm as a very good investment.

SIC had rented a factory to the company in 1970 and was owed some rent. The council was approached to intervene in 1975. A restructuring of the firm was arranged between the HIDB, SIC and other interests whereby the HIDB and the SIC both acquired equity while John West Ltd granted a substantial loan. The result was that the SIC and HIDB shareholding, along with another private British shareholding, made the company British-owned. This circumvented the exchange control problems of the firm whereby British financiers were prevented by the Treasury from converting sterling into Kroner for a loss-making investment. In addition, the company had a vastly increased risk capital base for future expansion and borrowing.

A second shareholding was provoked by the SIC's concern that the local economy was being endangered by the takeover of Shetland firms by large firms from outside Shetland. The danger was especially great for firms engaged in oil-related activity. The Council decided to intervene when a mainland company was considered to be taking over a lot of small firms in Shetland concerned with quarrying. The Council needed to ensure its own supply of aggregates for road-building as well as to ensure that other Shetland firms were not faced with a monopoly. As a result a joint company called Shetland Aggregates Ltd was formed by the Council and a Shetland entrepreneur experienced in this field.

The Council also set up a wholly-owned company, Zetland Finance Ltd, in order to raise money for the financial support of local industry which was affected in one way or another by oil developments. The company provided the machinery to raise money as cheaply as possible and to support the local economy as efficiently as possible. However, the company was not used to support local industry because it had to pay corporation tax on any profits. If, instead, the Council invested directly in a firm by using the special 'disturbance allowance' that the oil companies were paying the Council, as it had done with Shetland-Norse Ltd, the Council paid no tax on its investments because of the different tax status of local government.

When Nottinghamshire and Greater Manchester PTEs invested in Horizon Midlands their objective was not to support economic development in the area directly. Nottinghamshire's involvement came about mainly because of its concern about public expenditure on the East Midlands airport. Horizon Midlands Ltd provided inclusive air holidays and acted as a travel agent. It operated from the East Midlands Airport at Castle Donnington, near Derby, and also from Elmdon Airport, Birmingham In January 1974 Court Line Ltd took over the shareholding of Horizon Holidays Ltd after Horizon Holidays hit financial difficulties. The major asset of Horizon Holidays was the subsidiary, Horizon Midlands. But in August 1974 Court Line itself ceased trading. The problem for Horizon Midlands was to convince investors that *it* was still solvent despite the collapse of Horizon Holidays and then Court Line. Trading in the shares of Horizon Midlands was suspended twice in 1974 in order to protect it.

The liquidator for Court Line was concerned to realise the highest price for the Horizon Midlands asset. Horizon Midlands together with the merchant bankers, Hill Samuel, got together a consortium to make a bid for Court Line's 58 per cent holding in Horizon Midlands. An offer of 14p. per share was turned down. Subsequently Rumasa Ltd, a Spanish firm concerned with wine production, banking and hotels, offered something around 18p. However, Rumasa was not prepared to bid for all the shares which, under Stock Exchange rules, they were required to do if buying more than 30 per cent of the shares of a public company. The Stock Exchange's Takeover Panel advised the liquidator against the offer. At the same time Horizon Midlands' own consortium fell apart. Hill Samuel then decided to approach various local authorities with a financial interest in the airports in the Midlands. At the time, 60 per cent of Horizon Midlands' 'Inclusive Tour' traffic was handled through the Birmingham airport and 40 per cent through East Midlands Airport. In East Midlands' case this represented about a quarter of the total passenger throughput of the airport. The collapse of Horizon Midlands would have had a considerable impact on both airports.

Horizon Midlands approached the West Midlands County Council (whose area includes the Birmingham airport) and the East Midlands Airport joint committee, comprising Derbyshire (responsible for $\frac{4}{9}$ ths of the airport's liabilities), Nottinghamshire ($\frac{3}{9}$ ths), Leicestershire ($\frac{1}{9}$ th), and Nottingham City ($\frac{1}{9}$ th). West Midlands County Council explored the possibility of its West Midlands PTE entering the consortium under powers contained in the 1968 Transport Act. They decided amongst other things that they did not have the powers to get involved since Horizon Midlands was not a 'necessary and conducive part' of the work of the PTE. They also thought that the same limitations applied to Section III of the 1972 Local Government Act which enables a local authority to do anything calculated to facilitate the discharge of its functions. Only Nottinghamshire remained interested. At the same time Lancashire United Transport Ltd (LUT), a company associated with the Greater Manchester PTE, and later taken over by it, also expressed an interest. LUT, prompted by Greater Manchester PTE, wanted to invest in tour operations because of the beneficial effects this might have on its coaching operations.

A new consortium was founded and the liquidator accepted its offer of 16p. The 58 per cent was then offered to existing shareholders. After take-up this left 27 per cent of issued share capital for the consortium. Nottinghamshire and LUT insisted on having 10 per cent each. Since they were the major bodies on the consortium they had to have priority. They also wanted directors on the board. The existing board stated that they would have to own around 10 per cent in order for this to be acceptable. In the end, Nottinghamshire and LUT acquired their 10 per cent each. Later Greater Manchester PTE also bought a 4 per cent stake, so making its direct and indirect holding 14 per cent. This facilitated an interest by the GMC PTE in air tour activities as well as keeping abreast with developments concerning coach operations. In other words, the sharehold-ing by Nottinghamshire and Greater Manchester were for public expenditure reasons and transport expansion reasons respectively, not directly for local economic development reasons. The PTE used powers under the 1968 Transport Act and Nottinghamshire used a section of the 1972 Local Government Act empowering it to spend a proportion of the rates in the interests of its area.

In the case of Blackburn Football Club the council also wanted to help float a share issue. The club had made a loss three years out of five between 1969 and 1973, and the accumulated losses had risen fourfold. Shares were acquired by the Council as a token gesture to assist in the promotion of the sale of shares. No explicit powers to subscribe for shares were thought necessary. The purpose of keeping the club going was to help promote the advertisement of the town as a suitable area for investment. Again, as with Nottinghamshire's involvement in Horizon Midlands, the support for the company could only be of indirect assistance to investment in the area.

West Yorkshire PTE supported some coach and tour-operating firms in its area for reasons similar to those giving rise to Greater Manchester's involvement in Horizon Midlands, to establish a stake in supporting a possible growth area in transport provision which provided marketable, profitable commodities. In South Yorkshire the PTE bought Booth & Fisher (Sales and Service) Ltd as part of a purchase of the Booth & Fisher bus-operating group, most of which was fully integrated into the PTE itself and not retained as a separate company. The sales and service company was kept separate by the PTE and was to be retained by the PTE so long as it remained profitable. London Transport set up a consultancy company to market abroad its expertise in transport engineering and to undertake consultancy and construction contracts where possible.

In addition to these investments by local authorities and PTEs there were two proposals for shareholding in manufacture and commerce which local authorities were proposing at the end of the ten-year period under examination. In 1976 South Yorkshire County Council set aside £2m., or 5 per cent of its superannuation fund for direct investment in small profitable companies which provided employment in South Yorkshire and the surrounding area. The County Regional Investment Scheme, as it was known, was operated under the Local Government Superannuation Regulations 1974 which allowed local authority funds to invest up to 10 per cent of their holdings in unquoted securities. The Scheme was seen as 'a logical extension of the fund's activities at a time when many of the smaller companies in the UK were frustrated in their investment programmes through their inability to secure sufficient capital'.[1] The proposals were a response to what were seen as the problems facing smaller companies in the South Yorkshire area, and were an attempt to support the development of the local economy particularly in the case of firms with less freedom of manoeuvre in the capital markets. The scheme was primarily aimed at taking equity stakes in smaller companies; no investment was to give control to the Council, but holdings were to be large enough to ensure the views of the fund's advisors were taken into account by the directors of the company.[2]

In 1977 London Transport proposed the formation of a bus-manufacturing company along with the other PTEs and British Leyland, as we described in the Introduction. The primary objective for the PTEs was to guarantee bus supply, but the company would also have contributed towards GLC policy of encouraging employment and investment in London.

As is to be expected from the absence of systematic legal provisions, the local authority support for new or existing local enterprises encompass various types of companies and objectives, and involvement in these is very small. When we discuss local and regional authority support for manufacturing and commerce we will therefore be referring largely to activity at the regional level.

III LAND DEVELOPMENT AND INFRASTRUCTURE: THE LOCAL BACKGROUND

We will deal firstly with shareholding for development purposes, and then go on to discuss shareholding for infrastructure purposes. Both these aspects of local authority shareholding are concerned, to a greater or lesser extent, with the facilitation of development within the local authority's area, the protection or improvement of the local economy and the reduction of state expenditure. These shareholding schemes are summarised in Table 3.2.

In Norwich, the objective of setting up the Colegate Companies in 1972 was to facilitate the development of a derelict industrial site near the city centre primarily for luxury housing; it was part of Council policy to convert such sites wholly or partly into residential areas to increase the attractiveness of the city for further private investment. The Council also wanted to preserve the historic buildings on the site, and to improve the river frontage. The particular area in question, at Friars Quay, had not been developed because it was back-land and because it was only attractive to private developers for office development, and not for the residential development which was favoured by the local authority. The Council eventually decided to form two joint companies with a local builder in order to promote the development of the site in accordance with its policy objectives. Carters, the private developer in the scheme, would not have been interested if the development risks had not been shared with the local authority. In order to set up the companies the Council used a 1920 Local Act which contained fairly broad ancillary powers.

Similarly, in 1973, the same Council acquired some 500 acres of land outside the city centre, partly using extra money provided under Department of the Environment Circular 102/72 and partly using 'key sector' money. They decided to develop this land for mixed residential purposes, including council housing, private houses and housing association dwellings, together with shops and associated community provision. This development was intended to take place in three 'villages', to be developed successively over a period of from ten to fifteen years. A small piece of land near the centre of the first of those 'villages' was felt to be unattractive, by reason of its size, to a private developer for residential purposes, yet the Council was keen to promote private housing on that site. It set up its own company to raise money and manage the development, using Section III of the 1972 Local Government Act after a central government statement that this section could be used to acquire shares for development purposes.

In Manchester a major part of the city centre was to be developed by Town and City Properties and the Prudential Assurance Company. The site was to contain large shopping stores (over 1m. square feet), 200 shops and some offices (200,000 square feet), provided by the developer, and a market hall, a multi-storey car park (1800 cars), and a bus station, provided by the City Council. The shopping centre was to be the largest in Britain, and to act as a counterbalance to other regional shopping centres in the North-West. In 1970–1 the Prudential found that it could not

TABLE 3.2 Local and regional authority shareholding in land development and its infrastructure

Local authority (a) Land development	Name of company, % and date of shareholding	Objects of company and local or regional authority interest
Norwich D.C.	Colegate Developments Ltd and Colegate Investments Ltd, 50% of voting shares, 1971	To redevelop an area on the edge of the city centre for mixed uses, and to control the timing and quality of the redevelopment
	Conesford Developments Ltd, 100%, 1975	To develop an area which was too small to attract the private sector, for private housing on the outskirts of the city
Manchester D. C.	Manchester Mortgage Corporation Ltd (plus subsidiary Second Manchester Mortgage Corp. Ltd), 100% 1972	To help finance an enlarged, profitable city centre redevelopment which the private sector, by itself, would not undertake
Brighton D. C.	Brighton Civic Development Co, Ltd, 50% of voting shares, 1973	To build a conference, exhibition and entertainments centre in the city centre because the market, if left to itself, would have attracted other uses, e.g. offices
Birmingham D.C.	National Exhibition Centre Ltd, 50%, 1970	To manage the construction and operation of the National Exhibition Centre

Local authority proposals

| Greater London Council | 1977: Earls Court Exhibition Centre: in conjunction with British Rail and Town and City Property Co. to improve facilities and extend exhibition centre 1977: Inclusion in General Powers Bill of a clause enabling the Council to acquire shares in construction companies to facilitate completion of council contracts | |

Local authority (b) Infrastructure	Name of company, % and date of shareholding	Objects of company and local or regional authority interest
Buckinghamshire C.C. and Aylesbury Vale D.C.	Buckingham Borough Development Co. Ltd, 51% and 49% of share capital respectively, 1971	To assemble and service land for predominantly private housing in furtherance of town expansion, in an area otherwise unattractive to developers
Shetland Islands Council	Grandmet Shetland Ltd, 50%, 1974	To monitor the impact of a construction workers' village and its facilities
	Shetland Towage Ltd, 50%, 1975	To provide and manage tug and other related port facilities
	Sullom Voe Association Ltd, 50%, 1975	To control the design and construction of the Sullom Voe port, pipe laying and oil storage facilities, in a continuous manner
Southend D.C.	Thames Estuary Development Co. Ltd, (plus subsidiaries Maplin Development Co. Ltd and London Maplin Rail Link Ltd), 18%, 1968	Planning and management of land reclamation and other facilities for airport and oil terminal at Maplin

Local authority PTEs

Greater Manchester PTE	Lancashire United Transport and subsidiaries, 1975	To integrate stage carriage operations
	SELNEC Transport Services Ltd, 1971; both wholly-owned companies	To obtain tax advantage of group relief schemes

Local authority PTEs	Name of company, % and date of shareholding	Objects of company and local or regional authority interest
West Midlands PTE	Pearson Green Ltd and W. Midlands Passenger Transport Ltd; both wholly-owned, 1972 and 1973	To claim capital grants To provide service conditions structure for staff transferred from a Midland Red undertaking
Tyne and Wear PTE	Tyneside Transport Services Ltd, wholly-owned, 1972	To obtain tax advantages of group relief schemes
Merseyside PTE	Merseyside Passenger Transport Services Ltd, wholly-owned, 1972	To obtain tax advantages of group relief schemes, and later to enter into group leasing arrangements with Greater Manchester and Tyne and Wear PTEs
All PTEs	National Transport Tokens Ltd, 40%, 1972	To provide a travel token system to facilitate public passenger travel within the UK

Local authority proposals

Tyne and Wear Metropolitan C.C.	1976: Proposal to acquire shares in company for the development of the Tyneside Metro.	

finance the whole scheme. Other financial sources were approached unsuccessfully by Town and City and by the City Council, which regarded the development, Arndale Centre, as a means of promoting Manchester's economy. Other financial sources approached thought that the cost of the Centre, £30m., was too high for one site in one provincial city. The Council did not have enough money in its locally determined sector allocation (expenditure on central area redevelopment, car parking, offices, sports centre, etc., which does not require individual loan sanctions) to finance the development itself. It acquired two companies which were instrumental in raising money to facilitate development of the Arndale Centre. First, using a 1971 Local Act, the Council acquired a 'shell' company for £100 (Michelhurst Ltd) and renamed it the Manchester Mortgage Corporation Ltd (MMC). The share capital was increased to £1·5m. £450,000 of this was then used to acquire Pallas Finance and Developments Ltd from S. G. Warburg, merchant bankers. This company was renamed the Second Manchester Mortgage Corporation (2nd MMC). By acquiring this company MMC could raise money on the stock market by a loan stock issue. 2nd MMC qualified for trustee status under the Trustee Investments Act because it had (under its former name) paid a dividend on its share capital for each of the five preceding years. The guarantee of interest by the Council meant that the loan stock issue could be floated at a lower interest rate than that prevailing for speculative developers at the time. The issue of £5m. loan stock was in fact oversubscribed. Construction began in April 1972 and was due to be completed in 1978. In 1976 the company raised a further £13·5m., this time in the form of bank loans owing to the lack of buoyancy of the stock market.

Brighton's formation of a company was also to raise money. In 1973 the Council wanted to build a conference centre with exhibition and entertainments facilities on part of the five acre Churchill Square Development site in the city centre. It was to be the largest centre of its kind in Britain, incorporating the latest designs in audio-visual aids, simultaneous interpretation equipment, and press and TV facilities. If the site had not been used for a conference centre it would probably have been the subject of a private planning application for office development because of its central location.

The conference industry has historically been important to Brighton and is mentioned in the Interim Statement on Policy for Tourism in the Structure Plan as a major industry. Brighton was one of the few resorts to employ staff specially for this purpose, and it created a lot of spin-offs for the town. Its conference facilities attracted the major political parties, trade unions and business from abroad. The local authority's Resort and Conference Services Department actively promoted the advantages of Brighton for conferences to attract business as far afield as Bolivia and Puerto Rico.

The problem in developing a new conference centre was raising finance to pay for it. The Council had bought the land for the conference centre under Compulsory Purchase Order, but did not want to dispose of it to a developer as this would have meant notifying the Department of the Environment under the disposal provision for compulsorily acquired land, and the Department of the Environment may not have allowed a disposal for such purposes. Therefore, funding had to be found while the Council remained owner of the land. The local authority was unable to find £20m. itself so a company was formed to raise the money in the first instance, the money to be repaid over a thirty-year period to the lenders. The company raised the money from a consortium of banks on the security of the obligation of the local authority to pay it back over the thirty-year period. Guinness Mahon, which provided most of the money, owned the company jointly with the Council, although technically only two Councillors were involved. The Council itself had been reluctant to use its Local Act empowering it to acquire shares because permission from the Department of the Environment was required and it was again feared that they would object to the development. As a result two Councillors, rather than the Council, formed the company.

Birmingham formed a joint company in order to expedite the construction of a project. In 1969 a joint committee of Birmingham City Council and the Birmingham Chamber of Industry and Commerce had been set up to examine ways in which the prosperity of the city could be improved. The Council was concerned about the effects of the depletion of industry from the city, which it attributed largely to regional policy. In the course of discussion it was decided to bid for the location of the national exhibition centre in Birmingham. The Council and Chamber of Industry and Commerce were successful in this. It was considered very important that the centre be constructed as quickly as possible to have the maximum impact and spin-offs for the local economy. It was estimated that the exhibition centre would generate 6–9000 jobs in the Birmingham area. The centre itself created 3250 jobs in catering, maintenance and associated employment.

The project was to contain seven exhibition halls (1m. square feet – about the size of Olympia and Earls Court combined), parking space for 15,000 cars and 200 coaches, and offices, shops, restaurants and other supporting facilities. The whole process of construction, planning approvals, financing, design and public enquiry was to take five years from the acquisition of the land. By the end of 1972 the general contractor for the development had been appointed through competitive tender. The Council and the Chamber of Commerce formed a joint company to manage the development and running of the centre in order to ensure completion on target, the Council using its 1959 Local Act which contained specific provisions for the exhibition centre.

In 1977 there were two GLC proposals put forward in the land development category. The first one invoved the GLC in acquiring an equity stake in the Earls Court Exhibition Centre to improve the facilities of the Centre and to extend its size in cooperation with Town and City properties and British Rail. The GLC was concerned about the drift of exhibitions away from London to the other local authority supported centre, just outlined above, the National Exhibition Centre in Birmingham. Like Birmingham Council, the GLC realised the indirect economic effects of an exhibition centre on the local economy.

The second proposal from the GLC was to acquire equity in construction companies for which the council was having to pay extra-contractual amounts of money in order for the companies to complete council building contracts. The Council's 'objective in obtaining [the necessary] legal powers was simply to assist the council in minimizing the cost to the ratepayers of providing financial assistance to contractors who, because of extreme financial difficulties, would otherwise be unable to complete council contracts'.[3] The GLC considered equity would provide financial support with the possibility of some return if the financial position of the contractor subsequently improved. At the same time it would improve the capital structure of the firms. The Council would be able to achieve its objective of minimising public expenditure if there were such a mechanism for securing the return of its extra-contractual payments by treating them as investments.

When we examine local shareholding which was concerned with infrastructure provision we find it is often closely related to land development. In a number of the cases, local authorities were to overcome or minimise public infrastructure costs which could not be paid for out of public expenditure and therefore prevented other development from taking place. In other cases the concern of local authorities was to reduce the impact on public expenditure as well as any detrimental local economic impact of developments which were going ahead anyway. Or, finally, the local authorities were just concerned to obtain some income from private sources to use on general infrastructure support.

In 1964 a new town was proposed for the North Buckinghamshire area, to be built outside the New Towns Act provisions, and for four towns to be expanded in the area to accommodate some of the predicted rapidly growing population in South-East England. Draft plans for the town expansions were completed in 1965 and Buckingham was one of these. In 1966 it was decided that the new town would be built under the New Towns Act provisions and work was subsequently begun on Milton Keynes; the town expansion plans were unchanged. An informal plan for Buckingham's town expansion scheme was prepared in 1966 by the Council and approved by the Minister. The area in question was intended to accommodate an additional 10,000 population, comprising 350 acres on six green field sites extending around the town. The plan was for housing and industry, with a mix of housing types ranging from luxury private housing to council housing.

At the height of a boom period in the property market, private enterprise had not ventured into the process of assembling land for development on the edge of Buckingham where the Council had designated the town expansion sites. A large capital expenditure was required on a ring road and new sewage works to service these sites, and there were plenty of sites elsewhere for private initiative, especially in office development, which would not involve such an initial outlay. Buckingham was the drainage authority at the time and did not wish to bear the full costs of this infrastructure itself by putting a heavy burden on the rates. Eventually, the Councils concerned formed a joint company together under the provisions of a 1971 Local Act, and the company entered into an option agreement with landowners in the area in order to facilitate the assembly of land and the provision of infrastructure. Under the option agreement the company paid £500 per acre to exercise an option to purchase land within five years. A further sum of £3500 per acre was paid when the option was exercised and the freehold interest of the land passed to the company. This price was relatively low because the lack of infrastructure made the land less desirable to developers. When the land was sold by the company, the landowner would be entitled to a further payment depending on the price received for the land. The further payment would consist of 75 per cent of the money remaining after the company had paid all relevant expenses of the appropriate phase of the development, including the cost of infrastructure, service charges, purchase monies, administration and expenses.

The three phases of development were each to be linked to a phase of sewage works construction, and each phase was to be taxed and administered separately. Initially the Borough Council was to borrow money for the sewage works, though a new arrangement was negotiated with the Anglian Water Authority after they had taken over responsibility for drainage in the area in 1974. The Council was to apply to the Department of the Environment for loan consent for each phase and this would be reimbursed by the company except for the proportion relating to areas not included in the scheme. The company would pay for the sewage works out of the profits from the scheme. The outer ring road was to be paid for and constructed by the housing developers where it directly adjoined a housing development site. All ring road links between housing areas would be paid for and constructed by the County Council as highway authority.

Southend Council was also concerned to promote a development and to minimise the costs of infrastructure provision but in this case it was also concerned to introduce planning considerations which would minimise the harmful effects of the development on the local economy. In 1968 the Roskill Committee of Inquiry was examining the siting of the proposed third London airport. One of the sites it was considering was the Foulness area off the Essex coast near Southend. Some private companies formed a consortium to promote the idea of reclaiming Foulness for the airport. Southend Council also wanted to promote the idea, provided certain local planning considerations were taken into account, because of the benefit to the town that would accrue from having an airport at Foulness. The Council as planning authority was concerned about the proximity of the airport to the coast, the orientation of the airport, and access to London and elsewhere. It did not want to become involved in considerable public expenditure compensating for inadequate provision of access by private developers building in a relatively haphazard manner, and it did not want the location of the airport to damage the local tourist industry. So the Council bought an 18 per cent share of a consortium company which also included Shell, Rio-Tinto-Zinc and Town & City, amongst others. Like Nottinghamshire the Council used the general power to spend a small proportion of rates money in the general interests of the area.

The Shetland Islands Council became involved in companies for similar reasons to Southend. The area selected by the SIC for processing and storing oil to be brought ashore was at Sullom Voe. The site chosen was hilly with no existing road access. This made construction more difficult and expensive.[4] However, it was one of the Council's objectives to influence the oil developments in order to minimise their disruptive effect. Given this objective, the site chosen at Sullom Voe contained the following positive points:

1 the area was adequate in size and there was adequate shore line for jetties with ready access to deep water;
2 there was a minimum of land above a certain standard for other uses;
3 there was no population;
4 the rock structure in the south of the area could possibly be used for cavern storage of oil, so reducing the requirements for surface tankage;
5 contours offered some opportunity to screen construction and permanent facilities;
6 the site was remote so minimizing interference with a near-by village during construction and operation;
7 the limited land access enhanced the security of the completed facilities.[5]

The Council was anxious to secure some continuing control of the planning and development of the oil terminal since it would eventually be asked to give planning permission for over £300m. of development at the terminal. These developments would involve facilities for stabilising the incoming crude oil, separating and converting the various gases and volatile liquids, and storing the oil and gas. The Council would thus secure the landing of oil at *one* site and would secure control over the landings at that site. In addition to empowering it to acquire the land involved quickly (pre-Community Land Act) the 1974 Zetland County Council Act gave the Council powers to subscribe for and take shares in any company or undertaking ancillary to its fairly broad development functions under the Act. A joint non-profit-making company was formed between the oil companies and the Council, to control the oil terminal developments. The Chief Executive claimed that the main purpose of the company – the Sullom Voe Association – was not financial. It was

> to ensure strong and continuing control over the developments. Normal planning controls demand from the Planning Authority almost divine fore-knowledge. To anticipate all eventualities and to form adequate conditions one must have a depth of knowledge greater than that of the developer. Even then, to enforce conditions is not as simple as to frame them. Involvement in the association would enable the council to remedy shortcomings and to fill gaps left by planning conditions.[6]

The main concerns of the Council were security against sabotage, pollution, environmental effects and effects on local communities. Each one of these concerns could have involved the Council in substantial expenditure if the development was not controlled.

Part of the process of transporting the oil once it had been brought ashore and processed at Sullom Voe was the loading of oil tankers and the navigation of the tankers into and out of the Voe. The Council was the Port Authority for the area and was responsible for constructing the jetties, harbours and related buildings. The recovery of the cost of this would come from the dues imposed on the tankers. There would also be a charge for tuggage and towage facilities. By forming a joint company with a Glasgow shipping consortium which also paid for half the council's share capital in the company, the Council would receive substantial revenue from the towage charges, and would have some influence over the safety and pollution problems which concerned it. It also wanted to be able to influence the employment of Shetlanders on the tugs.

The SIC also acquired shares in a company set up to manage the building and running of a camp at Sullom Voe. The construction of the terminal involved the initial recruitment of 1100 construction workers, mostly from outside Shetland. The Council was concerned about the impact of 1100 extra people on existing facilities and public services in an island with only 17,000 population. It decided that they should be encouraged to be as independent as possible by living in a specially constructed, high-quality camp, or 'village', at Firth near Sullom Voe. In order to ensure that the Council had a continuing influence over the camp, it formed a joint management company with a subsidiary of Grand Metropolitan Hotels Ltd. The oil companies paid for the construction of the camp and the Council received half the income from its management as well as having its share capital paid for by its partners in the company. The Council's main concern was that there should be no additional need for the public provision of facilities and services for the construction workers in order to protect the local economic and social structure.

Tyne and Wear County Council was also concerned to control public infrastructure costs. The Passenger Transport Executive and British Rail proposed a joint scheme for the construction of a Metro-transit system in the Tyneside area utilizing existing rail track and new track, and some underground. The system was to be part of an integrated urban transport system, serving largely the inner and central areas of Tyneside. However, the project seemed doomed because of cuts in public expenditure and a dispute between ASLEF and the TGWU on manning the new trams. In December 1976 the County Council received government approval for completion of the thirty-one-mile, £176m. rapid-transit system. The Transport Secretary stated that £32m. had already been spent, that it would cost £80m. to halt the project and little less than that to freeze it temporarily. There was also the need to boost employment on Tyneside. At the last minute the rail and bus unions came to an agreement over manning through the intervention of the TUC General-Secretary.

The PTE and British Rail would be setting up a joint operating company to develop and manage the system. The County Council would be liable for any excessive construction costs over £161m. and operating deficits of over £5m. a year, and was putting up 30 per cent of the money. As a result, it felt it wanted to influence the joint operation but under the 1968 Transport Act it could only issue instructions to its PTE on major policy issues and not on detailed day-to-day implementation. It therefore decided to use new local act powers to enable it to take part in the operating company. In 1977 the establishment of the company was still being negotiated.

Most of the other PTE involvement in companies was concerned with minimising public expenditure while maintaining services, or raising money from private sources to be used on general transport provision. In the case of Greater Manchester PTE, Lancashire United Transport Ltd was facing financial difficulties and it was in the PTE's best interests to buy the company rather than take over its activities itself because this would have involved expensive compensation payments to LUT. Roughly 75 per cent of its activities were in the original SELNEC area, with more than this in the new Greater Manchester area, and 10 per cent of all GM PTE's stage carriage activities were conducted by LUT. An operating contract was drawn up in 1971 between SELNEC and LUT as a first step in their involvement with the company. This guaranteed LUT continuous operations in their area. It also contained a proposal for the PTE to take over LUT eventually, which they were entitled to do under the 1968 Transport Act.

The takeover of LUT by the PTE was not possible until 1976 because of problems concerning the political acceptability of PTE ownership of a public company. Because of LUT's weak competitive position, Lanaten Ltd made a successful bid for LUT in 1973 (on the advice of the PTE)

borrowing money for the acquisition which was guaranteed by SELNEC.
An agreement was signed between LUT and Lanaten that enabled LUT
to provide bus services which were coordinated with SELNEC's own
network. After it was decided that the PTE would eventually take over
LUT, the latter acquired subsidiaries in 1974 – the White Swan Group of
freight operating companies. The PTE agreed to LUT acquiring this on
LUT management's recommendation, which was based on commercial
considerations. The PTE was also keen for the company to be profitable,
even though its own objectives were broader. LUT also set up a new
company itself, Palatinate Ltd, which used to be a freight-operating
company, and became a storage company. A further company owned by
LUT, Motorway Motels Ltd, had to be sold off as part of the agreement
because it was not a good financial investment.

Merseyside, Tyne and Wear and SELNEC PTE all formed companies
for group relief purposes. This mechanism involved the PTE setting up a
company in which a large private company (such as Whitbreads in the
case of Merseyside and SELNEC and Rothschilds in the case of Tyne and
Wear) owned preference shares. The preference shares amounted to 75 per
cent of the total share capital (ordinary plus preference) and so the
accounts of the PTE company could be consolidated in the large private
company's accounts for tax relief purposes, provided, of course, the PTE
company continued to make losses. The tax relief would then be shared
between the PTE and the large company. From 1974 the tax advantages
for group relief could no longer be obtained in this way. The companies
were then used in conjunction with one another to enter into group leasing
arrangements whereby materials and equipment could be obtained more
cheaply.

West Midlands PTE formed a company for similar purposes but, as well
as raising money from group relief provisions, they claimed capital
investment grants. Profitable bus operators could claim capital investment
grants, or tax relief on new investments. The PTE was unprofitable so
could not do this. Instead, the PTE formed a new company, Pearson Green
Ltd, in 1972 in partnership with Cadbury Schweppes Ltd, a company
making large profits. The PTE owned the 239 ordinary shares while
Cadbury Schweppes owned 760 cumulative redeemable participating
preference shares. This arrangement allowed Cadbury Schweppes to
claim the capital grants which were shared between the PTE and Cadbury
Schweppes, and it also enabled both companies to benefit from group relief
provisions. Again the mechanism came to an end in 1974 when the
Finance Act of that year changed the provisions of these claims so that only
the holders of equity capital were eligible. Like the other PTEs the
company was retained for leasing purposes.

West Midlands PTE also formed a company to enable it to retain the
service conditions structure of the staff of part of the Midland Red bus
company which it wanted to acquire. Staff would have lost pension rights

and other entitlements if they had been transferred directly from Midland Red to the PTE. Many would have left and the service would have been disrupted. Instead Midland Red set up a company to which the staff and the intended purchasers were transferred. The PTE then bought this company and changed its name.

All PTEs own shares in Transport Tokens Ltd. The first PTE stake was taken up in 1972. The purpose of the company was to provide a travel token system to facilitate public passenger travel within the UK. Some PTEs owned shares in the company but did not use the tokens themselves. They were involved in the company in order to monitor developments which may have been of use to them or may have affected them in various ways. Other shareholders included British Rail and the National Bus Company.

IV DIMENSIONS OF THE CATEGORIES

We can divide up our two sets of schemes according to various dimensions which are useful for further analysis: the objectives of the state shareholding, the percentage shareholding, the appointment of directors by the state, the large firms involved, the political parties involved.

The objectives have been described so far in terms of supporting firms, facilitating development, and avoiding public expenditure. A further concern is viability and profitability in all but some of the PTE companies which have to make a loss for tax purposes in order to secure some return for the PTEs, and in the case of the Sullom Voe Association.

The percentage shareholding varies enormously between companies. In the companies dealing with manufacture and commerce the percentage varies from an insignificant proportion (Blackburn) to 10 per cent (Nottinghamshire), to 50 per cent (Shetland Aggregates) and to 100 per cent (some NIFC companies). On the whole though, the companies in this category only have a minority state shareholding.

In the land development and infrastructure companies, the state usually has at least a 50 per cent shareholding and often 100 per cent. The exceptions are Southend (18 per cent), and the PTE involvement in National Transport Tokens (40 per cent altogether).

When we examine the appointment of directors by the local and regional authorities there is a similar difference between the categories. The manufacturing and commercial companies do not always contain a director (or directors) appointed by the state. In the local development and infrastructure companies usually at least half the board is appointed by the local authority. These differences are to be expected from the differences in the percentage shareholdings between the categories, and hence the degree of control of the companies by the local and regional authorities. However, there is not a linear relationship between percentage shareholding and number of directors. In the HIDB companies for example, a company with a 8 per cent shareholding may have a director appointed by the board, while a company with a larger percentage HIDB holding may not.

The development and infrastructure companies involve large private companies in the development scheme far more frequently than the companies in the other category. In the case of Southend, Manchester, Brighton, Shetland and most of the PTE companies, large companies such as Shell, Mowlem, Rio-Tinto-Zinc, Guinness Mahon, Town & City, Cadbury Schweppes and Whitbreads are involved as joint shareholders, financiers or developers. In the manufacture and commerce category, large companies are involved mainly when they take over a small company after the state has supported its growth. In the HIDB companies, four were taken over by Shell, Wimpey, Fitch Lovell and Scottish and Newcastle Breweries. In only two companies, Highland Trout and Scottish Sea Farms, was a large company involved as a shareholder; in these cases they were Booker McConnell and Imperial Metal Industries respectively.

Shareholding as a whole was mainly initiated by Labour-controlled councils, but there was also a large number of Conservative-initiated schemes, or schemes which had Conservative support. At the regional level the Labour Government of 1964–70 set up the HIDB and the Conservative Government of 1970–4 set up the NIFC. However, the Conservatives discouraged the use of shareholding by the HIDB during 1970–4, while the Labour Government of 1974 onwards did encourage the full use of the NIFC's powers as well as those of the HIDB.

We have begun to show how local involvement in companies for 'local' reasons relates to the national processes we outlined in Part I. Local reasons include the facilitation, influence or control of investment and development, the control of public expenditure and the protection and growth of the local economy. This involves varying degrees of ownership and control, varying degrees of large company involvement, and varying degrees of party support, the development sector being more state controlled, with more large company involvement and more support from both major political parties. The rest of Part II will show in more detail how the local and regional shareholding mechanism works.

4 Manufacture and Commerce

This Chapter will analyse in detail local and regional shareholding in companies concerned with manufacture and commerce. Like the following chapter which deals with the land development companies, it will be in two parts. The first will discuss aspects of state control in the companies, trying to show how shareholding differs from alternative methods of intervention and how it facilitates private investment in manufacturing and land development. The second part will show how state shareholding is structured organisationally to facilitate viability, and how it contributes towards making firms and projects profitable. We will be concerned in both parts of each chapter to demonstrate what control and profitability mean in concrete terms.

I FACILITATION, INFLUENCE AND CONTROL

The state has acquired equity in order to make a company viable and also to make it an attractive investment for private capital. The HIDB regarded grants and loans as one-off methods of financing which were increasingly inadequate by themselves. Grants and loans did not alter the capital structure of firms in such a way as to make them more attractive to private capital. No special directors were appointed when grant and loan support were given and by 1976 the HIDB had decided that equity was probably needed in all cases.

Through its shareholding the Board aimed to intervene in the total capital structure of a firm to assist it through a crucial period where it needed a better capital structure or capital for growth. Assistance in the form of equity reduced a firm's gearing ratio, often from an unacceptable level. In addition, where equity was provided special directors were often appointed to the company's board if a particular skill or specialism was needed in the field of finance, marketing or other activities which would benefit the firm. By 1976 the Board had appointed 11 directors to 8 of the 23 companies in which it had equity. The Board did not need majority shareholdings for these purposes. Sharing in a small part of a firm's risks with a minority shareholding helped the HIDB act as a catalyst for private investment in firms.

Board expenditure was met from both grant-in-aid and receipts (for example, loan repayments). By 1973 the limits of the total HIDB assistance were £150,000 for any one project or £300,000 with reference to the Scottish Office. Where equity was concerned, there was an upper limit of 40 per cent which the Board could acquire in any one firm. In exceptional circumstances a higher proportion of equity could be acquired with the permission of the Secretary of State. For instance, in 1977, after our research was completed, the HIDB acquired its first majority holding of 75 per cent in Lewis Stokfisk Ltd, a fish drying development in the Western Isles. Within its budget and rules there was technically no limit to the amount of money the Board could spend on equity, although equity was not to be considered as the primary instrument of assistance. Between 1968 and 1976 the proportion of its budget used for this purpose was small, at about 3 per cent. (See Table 4.1). Shareholding, however, entitled the HIDB to profits which could be reinvested in the Highland economy and used in addition to grant-in-aid.

Firms in which the Board owned shares were all small in size (the largest had 250 employees), reflecting the character of industrial experience in the Highlands. The Board once investigated the possibility of buying shares in a parent company which owned a subsidiary in the Highlands so that its shares could be used to assist the subsidiary. But it was advised against this due to the restrictions in the Board's Act.

Normally, firms made an application to the Board for financial assistance, though an approach could be made the other way round, and the Board also played an active promotional role by attempting to interest people in setting up a particular venture. The Board decided on the basis of the location of the firm, its activity, commercial potential, and the Board's own financial budget whether and how to fund the firm. Equity was acquired with the consent of the firm, though it was unusual for this to be refused. It was part of the arrangement with the Secretary of State for Scotland and the Treasury under which the Board's financial activity operated that the Board's powers to take equity should not be exercised in such a way as to force a company to accept conditions which were objectionable to it.

Shareholding in manufacturing and commercial companies gave the HIDB influence over industries as well as individual firms which were part of those industries. In the case of Clansman Holdings Ltd the HIDB was concerned to retain economic activity in the Outer Hebrides. One way was to help restructure the Harris tweed industry which had been suffering a decline due to foreign competition and overcapacity. Clansman Holdings had been formed in 1972 to bring together all the various aspects of the industry – except weaving – by the merger of two companies. In 1973 there was a further merger and the HIDB put £80,000 (including share capital) into the company in order to help the consolidation. After the company continued to make losses the HIDB intervened again. It laid

TABLE 4.1   Highlands and Islands Development Board: Annual Investments

	Grants	Loans	Equity	
1965–6		59,500[1]		Amounts of equity per
1966–7	71,166	510,938		annum refer to companies
				listed for that year as
1967–8	253,807	886,318		well as additional equity
				in firms from previous years
1968–9	561,384	1,038,638	2500	Shetland Hotels
1969–70	575,517	1,005,348	57,500	Scottish Sea Farms
				Lennon & Kean
				Caithness Glass
				Highland Colliery[2]
1970–1	481,649	678,410	42,624	Gateway West Argyll
				Manor Hotel
				Campbeltown Shipyard[2]
1971–2	872,182	971,697	111,500	Hi Fab
				Clansman Frozen Foods
				Clansman Holdings
1972–3	1,498,981	1,245,305	43,298	Jennifreeth
				J. Anderson
				Scottish Instruments
				N. Scottish Helicopters
1973–4	1,638,101	1,743,846	75,000	Cairngorm Sports
1974–5	1,629,923	2,289,623	16,300	UEG Trials
				Dunoon Ceramics[3]
1975–6	2,131,466	2,273,590	301,000	Castle Stuart
				Highland Trout
				Jacobite Cruises
				Mackenzie Supplies
				Maricult Flotation
				Shetland-Norse
				Thaneway

Source: **HIDB Annual Reports.**
[1]Figures unclear: could be grants or loans
[2]Preference shares only
[3]Cumulative preferred ordinary convertible shares.

Total cumulative expenditure *1965–76*	
Loans & Grants	*Equity*
22,455,791	649,722
	(3% of total)

down conditions for further support which included detaching some loss-making operations from the main business, selling off excess properties, changing management, ensuring that three banks and the ICFC would continue their support, and that the company could obtain sufficient credit rating with firms which supplied the wool. The HIDB then put in £100,000 share capital, and a £50,000 special grant, into an increased total share capital. This gave it 39 per cent of the equity. The chairman appointed by the HIDB then reported back to the Board every three months. The HIDB itself embarked on some market research among clothing manufacturers to discover the kind of cloth wanted. This was part of a continuing set of studies by a number of bodies into the reorganisation of the Harris tweed industry which ended in proposals for a concentration of the weaving process into 12 'mini-factories' rather than in 550 separate homes. This would have facilitated the introduction of double-width power looms which would help produce the cloth that manufacturers now wanted. The aim was to arrest the decline in the industry and to make it a more viable competitive force at a reduced level of output. Otherwise, it was forecast by the Harris Tweed Association, the HIDB, and the Transport and General Workers Union, that the decline (shown in Table 4.2) would continue, eventually leading to the extinction of island weaving.

TABLE 4.2   Employment and production: Clansman holdings

	1969 *Clansman Group*	*1976* *Clansman Holdings*
Mill force	387 (100%)	116 (43%)
Weavers	1200 (100%)	585 (1975) (49%)
Cloth yardage	6,310,000 (100%)	2,600,000 (1975) (41%)

As well as being involved in the restructuring of a traditional industry, the HIDB also became substantially involved in the growth of a new industry, fish farming. It acquired shares in Scottish Sea Farms Ltd (oysters) Highland Trout Ltd, Maricult Flotation Ltd (oysters), Thaneway Ltd (trout and salmon) and Gateway West Argyll Ltd (trout). This was its largest concentration of equity investments, followed by hotels and tourism. The encouragement of fish-farming arose from the Highlands and Islands natural resources: pollution-free water, moderate temperatures, sheltered lochs. Equity was appropriate because of the high risks involved in an industry with heavy expenditure on capital equipment and technology and with such long lead times. The lead time for salmon is 3–4 years, and for oysters 2–3 years, after which there is a significant return on investment; this return could be very high in terms of capital appreciation of shares. If this type of activity was left to large companies there was a danger that it would never get off the ground on such a scale. Large companies usually become interested once the firms are viable. Scottish Sea Farms has been taken over in this way by Fitch Lovell, and Gateway West Argyll by Shell.

In all companies in which the HIDB owned shares, the possibility of private capital supporting the venture alone was extremely remote. Often different sources had been tried, such as the ICFC, merchant banks and joint stock banks. The companies were considered to be too much of a long-term risk, except in the cases where ICFC gave financial support linked to HIDB support, such as in Clansman Holdings, Cairngorm Sports, Manor Hotel and North Scottish Helicopters. Joint-stock banks would often extend overdrafts for considerable periods but could do no more; this increased gearing problems for the firms concerned. Equity was therefore of central importance in financial planning for each firm, and in more strategic economic planning and restructuring for the Board.

In the case of the NIFC the advantage of influence and control through shareholding was made quite explicit in its annual reports. The NIFC distinguished between three kinds of firm for which financial support was needed: survival cases, which were companies with serious liquidity problems, partly due to civil unrest, which would have a serious affect on the economy if forced to close down; growth cases, which were established companies wanting to expand or take on new investment; and new industry attracted to Northern Ireland by the NIFC or set up by the NIFC.

The advantages of acquiring equity in companies were seen as differing, depending on the category of company involved, but there were common themes in all the categories.

In survival cases:

(a) equity as well as loans provided finance which other financial institutions were unwilling to provide;
(b) equity provided sufficient control for changes in the financial structure and the management and organisation of the enterprise to be made by the NIFC;
(c) equity provided an 'interest-free' loan which was particularly valuable in these cases.

In growth cases:

(a) equity reduced the firm's gearing ratio and therefore reduced its reliance on large loans and overdrafts on which regular repayments (including interest) had to be paid. This was valuable particularly when large investments were made for expansion purposes;
(b) equity provided sufficient control for any reorganisation by the

NIFC in order to achieve viability;

(c) equity helped provide a capital structure which was attractive to private capital.

In new industry cases:

(a) unlike the HIDB, the NIFC was involved directly in promoting new companies by setting them up itself. 100 per cent equity in these cases created an enterprise which did not exist previously. The NIFC aimed in the long-term to attract private capital into these companies by offering other parties the option to purchase at a later stage if they had a particular expertise to offer;

(b) equity gave the NIFC a continuing interest in the company's development.

In all these cases control and monitoring was usually facilitated by the appointment of NIFC directors. It was recognised in all cases that external influence on management might be necessary if long-term profitability was to be achieved. This enabled the NIFC to promote and achieve the most efficient organisation. For these reasons loan guarantees were not used as risk capital. Guarantees involved the liability of a lender without the advantages, in that no monitoring was possible. But the risk was just the same. In order to convince private entrepreneurs and investors about its commercial objectives, the NIFC insisted on its money being treated like private investment, stressing that public money should be safeguarded like any other, and a reasonable return on investments should be expected in exchange for participating in the risk capital of an enterprise.

Not only was the advantage of control through ownership of equity made more explicit in the NIFC when compared to the HIDB, but the general scale of financial activity and equity support was much larger. The government made £50m. available to the NIFC, comprising public dividend capital and loan capital. The loan capital was made available to firms at the same or slightly above the normal rate of interest; the public dividend capital was used for equity which was paid back on a flexible basis. It was anticipated that, should all moneys be exhausted (i.e. all tied up at once in loans and equity), more finance would be made available. There was no upper limit to the amount or percentage equity that could be purchased by the NIFC because the size of firm depended on the objectives of the particular case, and because equity was always considered an intrinsic part of a firm's capital structure and was used together with loans and loan guarantees in a 'commercial' manner. The NIFC never gave grants. Between 1972 and 1976 35 per cent of all moneys used by the NIFC was spent on equity and the rest on loans. (See Table 4.3). However, the percentage spent on equity rose from 17 per cent in 1972/3 to 54 per cent in 1975/6.

The companies that the NIFC supported were, on the whole, larger

TABLE 4.3 Northern Ireland Finance Corporation:
Annual Investments

	Loans[1]	Equity
1972–3	970,200	203,900
1973–4	4,914,611	1,413,368
1974–5	3,162,005	2,104,000
1975–6	1,723,442	2,048,900

Source: NIFC Annual Reports.
[1]Includes loan guarantee and preference shares.

Total cumulative expenditure 1972–6	
Loans	Equity
10,770,258	5,770,168
	35% of total

than the HIDB firms, but still characterised by owner-management. They employed larger amounts of capital, had larger turnovers and larger employment capacities (e.g. 1400 employees in the case of Ben Sherman Ltd). The maximum size of firm the NIFC could assist was determined by its objective of developing new ventures in the restructuring process. This meant it would not invest directly in a large company, but would set up a joint subsidiary with the large company if necessary.

Like the HIDB, the NIFC functioned at two levels. At the company level it operated commercially, closely monitoring and influencing assisted cases, and offering great flexibility in the forms of finance available; at the industry level it helped to increase the profitability and 'added-value' of Northern Ireland industry, and increased 'local influence' in Northern Ireland industry. The NIFC embarked on the restructuring of industries of fundamental importance to the region's economy, such as steel stockholding and beef production. Equity allowed fundamental control in the reorganisation of a sector. In the beef industry the NIFC set up a meat plant with meat producers on the basis of a 15 per cent equity holding and a director. The NIFC considered that where it had a plan for an industry or sector it often only had to purchase a minority stake in a firm by agreement and then use its influence. This particular plan was under negotiation with beef producers for a couple of years and only reached fruition when the Northern Ireland Development Agency took over from the NIFC.

In the engineering sector, the NIFC purchased nearly 50 per cent of C. Walker & Sons Ltd, a steel stockholding company. The purpose was to help ensure the continuity of supply and competitive prices of steel for Northern Ireland engineering companies. The NIFC invested a further £500,000 a year later and the company was able to supply steel at competitive prices and to guarantee supply during the 1974 steel shortage.

The NIFC was also involved in the clothing sector and in setting up new companies concerned with electronics and audio equipment. When NIDA took over from NIFC it inherited a broad assortment of investments. NIDA embarked on a policy of trying to group the holdings into a more logical structure. It also started negotiations with Harland & Wolff, Northern Ireland's largest employer, to identify new projects into which the firm could diversify.

In the case of local authority companies, such as Shetland-Norse Preserving, Shetland Aggregates, the PTE tour companies and Horizon Midlands, the implications of shareholding for influence or control were similar to the HIDB and NIFC shareholding. Horizon Midlands provides an interesting example of a minority shareholding, where Nottinghamshire County Council and Greater Manchester PTE helped launch a share issue for the company by taking part in a consortium of underwriters. In the end they did not have to take up as much as 10 per

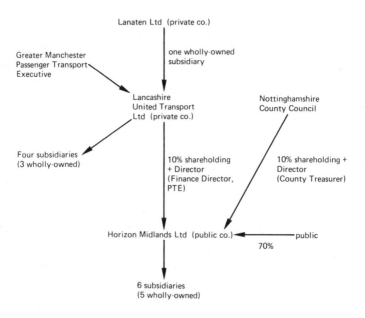

FIGURE 3   Horizon Midlands Ltd

In 1976 Greater Manchester PTE acquired Lancashire United Transport from Lanaten Ltd and also acquired a 4% stake in Horizon Midlands.

cent of the equity individually because the share issue had been so successful. But they both wanted 10 per cent in order to obtain a reasonable return on their investment. Greater Manchester also wanted a continuing interest in the company for its own purposes, in order to receive regular information on broader aspects of the travel industry. For this they needed a director and the existing board insisted that they would have to own around 10 per cent for this to be acceptable. At the end of the year in which Greater Manchester became involved, the company embarked on a new tour operation from Manchester airport in addition to its existing operations at Birmingham and East Midlands airports. It seemed that the interest of Greater Manchester PTE in the company had indeed developed to its advantage. In the case of Nottinghamshire the Council decided to appoint a director to Horizon Midlands because of its 10 per cent stake in the company, and to ensure that a member of the Council's staff would thereby have regular information on the progress of the company and some limited influence over financial details.

In Shetland Aggregates, the council controlled the company in order to ensure the supply of aggregates without the company being taken over, but by holding 51 per cent rather than 100 per cent of the shares, SIC could make use of private sector expertise in this particular undertaking. In Shetland-Norse SIC owned only 32 per cent of the equity, but appointed one director with extensive experience of Shetland traditional industries in order to monitor the firm and report back if anything significant arose.

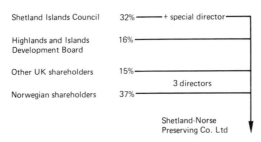

FIGURE 4   Shetland-Norse Preserving Co. Ltd

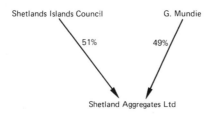

FIGURE 5   Shetland Aggregates Ltd

Sometimes there was a need for 100 per cent ownership because no private expertise was required. These 100 per cent owned companies included the PTE companies and Zetland Finance Co. (Shetland).

It must be remembered that the power or influence of directors is based on shareholding, not just on being a member of a decision-making board. An interesting contrast with the cases mentioned above is Manchester Ship Canal Co. Ltd, the company which operated the Port of Manchester. The City Council nominated most of the directors on the board of the company but did not have any share capital. The Council began support to the company in 1891 in the form of loans, since it was legally impossible for it to provide any other kind of financial aid. The loan agreement gave the Council the right to appoint the majority of the directors. The loan was made to enable the Ship Canal to be completed when public subscription failed to raise all of the £8m. authorised share capital. The Council decided that the completion of the canal was 'a matter of vital importance to the people of Manchester'. By 1970 it had lent the company over £10·5m. but owned none of the £4m. share capital.

From time to time the Council influenced company financial policy in order, for example, to eliminate extravagant expenditure. But it was very difficult for the Council to ensure repayment of its loans as quickly as it wanted. In 1959 the company did not agree to a Council request to redeem some of the Council's stock, despite an earlier obligation on the company to form a sinking fund out of revenue to redeem some of the debt. The Council was still receiving 3·5 per cent interest on its loan, which was much less than it could have obtained elsewhere. At the same time the company paid a dividend on its shares of 4 per cent for 1954/5, 5 per cent for 1956 to 1962, and 7 per cent for 1963/4. The build up of company assets had been largely due to the Council's loans, but the main people to gain financially were the shareholders, since the rate of return on the relatively small share capital (£4m. out of a total £22m. share and loan capital) worked out at a very high figure, especially when the rate of interest on the loan capital was uncompetitive. Without being a shareholder it was therefore difficult to influence certain decisions, especially where the rights and interests of shareholders were concerned. The unusual situation in the Canal Company where the Council could appoint a majority of the directors (11 out of 21 by 1970, the chairman still being a shareholders' appointee) gave the Council considerable influence over general financial policy, since this was in the shareholders' interests anyway. But it is interesting to observe how the shareholders' interests were protected even further on issues which involved disagreement with the Council. In company law directors cannot serve one particular interest unless by so doing they are acting in the best interests of the company. This should usually result in being to the advantage of shareholders.

The power of shareholding is the risk element; loans are secured on assets (usually) while shares are not, and loan stock holders are paid before shareholders in the case of company bankruptcy. Since they take a more substantial risk than other providers of finance, shareholders can appoint the directors. However, the degree of control associated with this right varies substantially depending on the size of shareholding and the size of firm. In large companies there may be thousands, even millions of shareholders, each with a minimal influence as an individual.[1] Blackburn Council was one of thousands of shareholders in Blackburn Rovers and had no continuing influence over policy. But nevertheless, minority shareholding above a certain level, such as 5–10 per cent of the share capital, can carry significant influence. Horizon Midlands had hundreds of shareholders owning over 70 per cent of its share capital but the two local authorities involved in the company had significant influence with 10 per cent holdings. In a public company with such a large number of shareholders, a 30 per cent stake is recognised to be sufficient sometimes to gain absolute control because the remaining shareholders take no active part in policymaking. The Stock Exchange takeovers and mergers code states that a shareholder with 30 per cent or more of the voting shares in a public company must make an offer to buy the remaining shares at the same price as others bought in the previous twelve months[2] because of the danger that a 30 per cent holder could attain control without paying a market price for the company. We have already referred to this condition in Rumasa's bid for Horizon Midlands shares in the previous chapter.

In most of the firms examined, the situation was different. The firms were small and their shares were not bought and sold 'on the market'. People who put up the money did so in large amounts in relation to the total share capital. The shareholders are also usually involved in the management of the company, either through special directors, or in person. Owning 30 per cent or 10 per cent in a small company may therefore mean being one out of only a handful of shareholders, all of whom also manage the company and have a similar influence over company policy. One company that approached the HIDB for financial support eventually declined a small percentage of equity because of the opportunity it would give of splitting the other two shareholder/managers who would be left with 45 per cent of the equity each. This would give the HIDB virtual control over the company with a 10 per cent stake whenever the other two shareholders disagreed.

This might mean that small owner-managed companies in which the state owns a minority shareholding would be fraught with conflicts of interest, loss of private control, and so on. But this was not the case in the companies examined, since the interests of the state and the firm were the same – to create successful, viable firms, often so that they could eventually survive without state support. Differences of opinion were usually of an administrative kind and resolved without great difficulty. The occasions when different reactions occurred, with the HIDB for example, were on the few occasions when a firm faced liquidation or shutdown; the Board, being concerned about loss of employment, went to considerable lengths to try to salvage a firm before it was liquidated.

II COMMERCIAL INDEPENDENCE AND PROFITABILITY

Local and regional authorities have, through their shareholdings, attempted to secure the viability of firms which would have collapsed because of an inappropriate financial structure, or failed to grow because of a shortage of capital for new investment. The companies existed to make a profit, facilitated by the state's involvement, and steered by the state in certain directions. However, commercial viability where the state is concerned should be distinguished from commercial viability where private firms operate by themselves. In some cases profitability will take longer to achieve than private financial institutions would tolerate. Also, the achievement of profitability in firms assisted by the state must be examined in the context of the overall objectives of the state, which are to assist in the process of industrial restructuring and regeneration, with a limited amount of capital, and to achieve local planning objectives. In all cases where shareholding by these authorities occurred the firms involved were potentially (commercially) viable.

These companies needed to be removed from the day-to-day decision-making process of government in order to achieve sufficient independence and flexibility to operate as commercial entities within the market. The company form itself creates conditions which promote independence, and it facilitates the pursuit of particular objectives which are different from those of local and regional authorities as a whole. A company is bound by the restrictions in the Company's Acts and must aim to be profitable in order to be credit-worthy. If insolvent the company can be voluntarily or compulsorily liquidated, or put in the hands of a receiver. All company accounting is carried on separately within the firm to maintain solvency and profitability, and all decision-making concerning the production and sale of commodities is made by the company's board.

In the majority of cases where shareholding has occurred in manufacturing and commerce, the state owns a proportion of the share capital of a firm, rather than the total share capital. This enables the firm to benefit from the commercial experience amongst the management and board directors in the private sector and allows the objectives of the state to be achieved without the need for the state to provide all the skills and expertise required to run a company, and without the need for it to become too heavily involved in the company's operations. In both the HIDB and the NIFC the original decision to invest in a company was always taken or approved by the boards of the two agencies. The boards also approved any further action which was subsequently required, especially where this involved financial support. But in both cases the companies were left to operate as independently as possible, with the two agencies providing a degree of continuing influence and monitoring.

Where the HIDB owns shares in companies, monitoring and influence is achieved in three ways which maximise commercial independence. Firstly, regular contact is kept with firms by one member of Management Services, part of the Finance Division. The responsibility of this person is to provide an 'after care' service to companies. The level of contact depends on the financial state of the company. Sometimes this means the HIDB officer attends all the company's board meetings, while at other times it means less frequent monitoring of the company's progress. Where the HIDB has invested a large amount of equity and loan capital and where it is anticipated that a long development period will elapse before profits are made, then a greater degree of involvement by management services usually occurs. This involvement comprises advice of a management and financial nature, and sometimes advice of a technical nature drawn from other Divisions of the HIDB.

Contact between the state and private firm is needed to protect the state's investment and to ensure that it is used in a particular way, but the degree of contact is kept to a minimum level in all cases. The type of contact taking place is no different from that available to any financial institution investing equity in a firm, and wanting to secure the best return possible. For example, regular contact is maintained between the HIDB and Maricult Flotation Ltd, an oyster hatchery in which the HIDB in 1975/6, invested £7000 of equity capital, and £40,000 of loan capital and grants. The firm had been involved in technical innovation in the development of this industry, which was regarded as having potential for larger-scale expansion in the Highlands and Islands, and the HIDB was prepared to wait until 1979 before any dividends were paid out of profits and until 1981 before full production was taking place. During this period regular monitoring by the HIDB took place so that it was able to offer additional assistance if the need arose, but it did not interfere in day-to-day management issues. Similarly an HIDB officer from Management Services kept in touch regularly with Hi-Fab Ltd, a steel fabrication firm specialising in aluminium parapets. Hi-Fab was created out of the assets of a liquidated company. The HIDB supported the new venture with equity, loans and grants and free rent for two years, and during this period of expansion when the capital structure of the firm was highly geared it monitored the progress of the company at least at monthly intervals. The company and all its operations were constantly open to the HIDB's inspection and the relationship between the HIDB and the company's owner-manager was informal. The HIDB and Hi-Fab were both interested in building up the firm until it was a publicly quoted Scottish company, and conflicts between the public and private sectors were only ever of a minor, administrative nature. However, the profitability of the company led to its takeover by Wimpeys.

Secondly, in addition to the contact with firms by Management Services, the HIDB sometimes appoints special directors to the boards of companies in which it owns shares. In all cases an agreement is made with the company (incorporated into the Memoranda and Articles of Association) to include this right. Special directors have been used particularly where some specialist skill was required which the HIDB could not provide itself from the usual monitoring by a Management Services Officer. Generally, special directors were chosen from outside the HIDB but occasionally an HIDB officer or Board member was appointed. Any director responsible for an equity holding must put the firm's financial interests first and foremost, so the use of special directors by the HIDB was intended to ensure that viability was achieved above all else. The HIDB was still able to monitor the situation because special directors made regular reports to the Board. Directors' reports on the progress of companies were frequently made available for meetings of the Board itself, especially where further action was required.

The HIDB appointed four out of twelve directors on the board of Cairngorm Sports Development Co. Ltd, in which it held 40 per cent of the share capital. It was agreed that two of the existing directors would be HIDB nominees, and two others were nominated for their special knowledge and useful contacts. The company was concerned to improve the skiing facilities at Aviemore and the HIDB became involved as part of its interest in promoting tourism in the Highlands. A large share of the equity was taken by the HIDB after a number of loans had been given because high capital costs were involved in improving the 'hill' with, for instance, chair lifts, and because returns on investment were low. The HIDB protected its share capital by making sure its special directors were capable of steering the company through negotiations with conservation bodies and tourist bodies, while at the same time aiming for commercial viability. Management services were involved hardly at all in the company's operations, and formal reporting back to the HIDB from the company occurred only bi-annually.

Thirdly, the HIDB also uses a combination of different types of contact. During some of the period when the HIDB held loan and equity capital in Caithness Glass Ltd, special directors were appointed by them to the company's board. At other times a close continuing influence of a specialist nature was maintained because an HIDB contact, respected for his reputation in glass marketing and exports, was on the company's management executive committee. While this situation lasted, a Management Services officer also attended board meetings to monitor the company's progress. This contact was necessary because, while the company was growing, the gearing ratio was constantly at a high level and the HIDB always had to be ready to inject more capital of one form or another when the need arose, as long as the company remained potentially profitable. Both types of contact were therefore essentially concerned with making the company profitable.

Like the HIDB, the NIFC and later the NIDA kept close links with companies in which they owned a portion of the equity, often through the use of special directors. However, the NIFC went further than the HIDB in ensuring that these directors were independent of the public authority. The directors were always selected from outside the NIFC to avoid any conflicts of interest between a director as a member of the company's board and as an officer of the public body. Special directors are considered necessary in many cases because the firms in which the NIFC and NIDA have invested are often small and lack the range of skills needed to grow. The task of finding appropriate persons for these appointments is difficult because firms approach the NIFC late, when their problems are acute, and because a high calibre of skill is needed to resolve these problems. A rigorous sensitivity test is applied to each firm in which the NIFC is interested in investing to see what its potential profitability will be. Where the state cannot provide the skills needed to achieve this, no investment is made.

In a number of cases the NIFC and then increasingly the NIDA set up wholly-owned companies in order to introduce a new industry into an area to improve the industrial structure. Wherever possible the NIFC or NIDA attempted to encourage other investors in joint ownership of these projects because this brought with it private sector expertise of various kinds. However, where they were unsuccessful, particularly during the early years of a company's life, the state nominated all the board of the company, which then operated independently but with regular monitoring by the NIFC.

Where local authorities owned shares in companies the systems of monitoring and advising were less well developed than in the Highlands or Northern Ireland. In Blackburn, Nottinghamshire and Greater Manchester PTE nvestments were one-off in nature and not part of an expressed strategy for achieving local economic objectives. The Council's shareholding in Blackburn Rovers Ltd achieved the desired effect of attracting private capital at a time when new shares were needed, so no monitoring of the company's progress was needed. Nottinghamshire's and Greater Manchester PTE's shareholding in Horizon Midlands, however, were taken on the basis of continuing financial involvement in the East Midlands airport by Nottinghamshire, and the running of a transportation service by Greater Manchester. Therefore both councils nominated one director each to the board of Horizon Midlands. The directors received regular financial information on the company, but there was no need to refer issues back to the local authorities because once the share issue was launched no additional support from the authorities was needed. In both cases the only time the local authority itself was involved in the company's affairs was in the initial decision to invest. In the case of Nottinghamshire the decision was taken by the full Council, while in Greater Manchester the initial investment by Lancashire United Transport, with which the PTE was very closely associated, went ahead after the chairman of the Greater Manchester Transportation Committee had been consulted.

In Shetland the Council intends to acquire shares in many companies in future as part of its policy of preserving traditional industry in the area at a time when North Sea oil explorations are adversely affecting local industry, and in the expectation that oil developments would be relatively short-lived. The Council's Research and Development Department began to monitor traditional industries, believing that Shetland must produce commodities itself in the short and the long term. Shares have been acquired in two companies so far. In the case of Shetland-Norse Preserving Company Ltd the original decision to invest was approved by the Council on a Policy Committee recommendation and after that the Director of Research and Development was appointed to the company's board. Similarly, with Shetland Aggregates Ltd the Council wanted the possibility of some continuing influence over the company's operations while allowing the company to operate normally without Council interference in its day-to-day operations. In this case, where the Council owned 51 per cent of the share capital, the Council and private company appointed an equal number of directors to the board, the Council again appointing officers to these posts.

Where PTEs bought companies to develop efficient and integrated transport services in their areas, PTE directors were appointed to the companies' boards to provide a policy input from the relevant divisions of the PTE, such as Finance, Operations, Development, Personnel. This was the case with South Yorkshire PTE's investment in Booth & Fisher (Sales and Service) Ltd, West Yorkshire PTE's investment in Hanson Coach Services Ltd and Baddeley Brothers (Holmfirth) Ltd, and London Transport's investment in London Transport International Services Ltd.

The acquisition of shares by local and regional authorities in a company concerned with manufacture or commerce allows them to control or influence the overall policy of the company; as shareholder they have the right to take part in the policy decisions and this right is exercised through special directors nominated by the authority to the company's board or by officers who monitor the company's progress. As far as possible contact by these means is kept to a minimum and interference in the day-to-day running of the company is avoided. The main purpose of the state's shareholding and monitoring procedures is to make companies profitable. For this the state remains in constant touch with the companies' affairs so that additional action can be taken when it is required.

While profitability is the main objective, dividends or capital gains made by the state are a useful spin-off. The profits themselves enable a scheme to more than cover any costs incurred by the authority. Since Nottinghamshire and Greater Manchester PTE each took a percentage of Horizon Midlands, the company has paid large dividends to these authorities because of the high level of profits made. In the Highlands dividends accruing to the HIDB have been limited because many companies are small and still relatively new. Also, most were owner-managed and any profits made were likely to be reinvested in the company rather than paid out in dividends. By 1976 only two firms had paid a dividend on share capital to the Board, but significant capital gains were made by the sale of shares of successful or potentially successful companies (five sales to Wimpeys, Shell, Scottish and Newcastle, Fitch Lovell and Management Aviation). In 1976 the HIDB looked for ways of making a better commercial return on its investments; instead of acquiring ordinary shares (with no automatic entitlement to dividends), it began to acquire convertible preferred ordinary shares so that a cumulative dividend must be paid. But it retained voting power if the company fell into arrears.

The return on capital employed for the firms where the state has shares gives an indication of the level of success obtained through this interventionist medium. (See Table 4.4.) However, the actual return for any one firm is only a rough guide to profitability because the average return varies between large and small firms, between and within different sectors of industry, and over time. Smaller companies are thought to have a generally higher return than larger companies. Bolton reported that the average return for small 'quoted' companies in 1954–63 was 18.6 per cent, while that for all quoted companies was 16.5 per cent. Small unquoted companies with fewer than 25 employees had a median return of 18 per cent. Those with more than 25 and less than 200 had a median return of 17 per cent. The variation between sectors is greater, with manufacturing companies in 1973–4 having a return of 23 per cent while consumer goods companies had 34 per cent, though these figures came from a different source[3] and it is difficult to tell whether comparable indicies are being used.

Within the manufacturing sector variations are again very wide. For example, in the pottery and glassware industry, where the HIDB has shareholdings, during an annual period between January 1975 and June 1976 in a sample of 9 firms the return on capital for Denbyware was 32.8 per cent compared with 9.6 per cent for Royal Worcester, while the median was 19.2 per cent.[4] These are large companies, unlike Dunoon Ceramics and Caithness Glass, but notwithstanding the difficulties of making comparisons, Caithness Glass's 23 per cent return in 1975 and Dunoon Ceramics's 46 per cent in 1976 appear to compare favourably.

Similarly, in the textile industry, from a sample of 17 firms during a period between September 1974 and June 1976 the annual return for John Haggas was 33.9 per cent while that of John Foster was only 2.9 per cent, with three companies registering a nil return and a median of 12.6 per cent.[5] Clansman Holdings, with HIDB equity, recorded a nil return, but with this range amongst large firms it would clearly be difficult again to assess how unfavourable this was. In the hotel industry, the range of

TABLE 4.4 Local and regional shareholding, private capital and financial return (manufacture and commerce)

Local and regional authority	Local and regional authority shareholding		Private capital (share and loan capital £)	Pre-tax profit (return on capital employed) (most recent figures)	Return to the authority
	amount £	proportion			
		%		%	
Nottinghamshire and Greater Manchester PTE					
Horizon Midlands Ltd	70,000	10	1.1 million	91	Dividend + threefold increase in share value
Shetland					
Zetland Finance Ltd	10,000	100		not yet available	
Shetland Aggregates Ltd	127,500	51	122,500 (only share figures known)	not yet available	
Shetland Norse Ltd	8000	32	44,700		
Blackburn					
Blackburn Rovers Ltd	250	insignificant	190,000	nil	
South Yorkshire PTE					
Booth & Fisher (Sales & Service) Ltd	100	100		20	
West Yorkshire PTE					
Hanson Coach Services Ltd	100 (+ 300,000 loan)	100		nil	
Baddeley Bros Ltd	602	100	11,853 (pre-acquisition)	16 (pre-acquisition)	Dividend of 26p per share pre-acquisition
London Transport					
London Transport International Services Ltd	21	100		not yet available	

Local and regional authority	Local and regional authority shareholding		Private capital (share and loan capital £)	Pre-tax profit (return on capital employed) (most recent figures)	Return to the authority
	amount £	proportion			
Highlands & Islands Development Board Bands of Inverness	7500 (+24,500 loan and grant)	11·9 (reduced to 8)	200,000	36	
Cairngorm Sports Developments Ltd	75,000 (+38,000 debenture)	39·9	140,000	13	
Caithness Glass Ltd	40,000 (+40,000 loan and grant)	34	100,000	23	Dividend
Dunoon Ceramics Ltd	5000 (+39,000 loan and grant)	not applicable (shares can be converted to voting shares)	32,000	46	Dividend
Gateway West Argyll Ltd	9000 (+95,500 loan and grant)	29 ? (reduced to 9)	148,000	nil	Capital gain
Clansman Holdings Ltd	180,000 (+80,000 grant and loan) (+80,000 grant and loan)	30	600,000	nil	
Hi-Fab Ltd	8000 (+42,000 loan and grant)	40	22,000	27	Capital gain

TABLE 4·4 (continued)

Local and regional authority	Local and regional authority shareholding		Private capital (share and loan capital £)	Pre-tax profit (return on capital employed) (most recent figures)	Return to the authority
	amount £	proportion			
J. Anderson Ltd	5,000 (+10,000 loan)	31	88,000	liquidated	
Jennifreeth Ltd	11,000 (+10,000 grant)	36	40,000	liquidated	
Lennon & Kean Ltd	10,000 (+55,000 loan)	16	65,000	liquidated	
Manor Hotel Ltd	15,000 (+42,000 loan)	21·7	120,000	nil	
North Scottish Helicopters Ltd	10,000 (+50,000 grant)	20	69,000	26	Capital gain
Scottish Instruments Ltd	25,000 (+136,000 loan and grant)	25	120,000	nil	
Scottish Sea Farms Ltd	39,000 (+15,000 loan and grant)	25	160,000	nil	
Shetland Hotels Ltd	17,298 (+43,500 loan)	23	60,000	8	Capital gain
UEG Trials Ltd	11,300 (+120,000 loan and grant)	36	90,000	substantial, but unrecorded	
Castle Stuart Foods Ltd	15,000 (+45,000 loan and grant)	25	54,000	– too early	
Highland Trout Ltd	30,000 (+20,000 loan)	11	240,000	– too early	

Local and regional authority	Local and regional authority shareholding		Private capital (share and loan capital £)	Pre-tax profit (return on capital employed) (most recent figures)	Return to the authority
	amount £	proportion			
Jacobite Cruises Ltd	70,000	35	130,000	– too early	
Mackenzie Building Supplies Ltd	10,000 (+60,000 loan)	25	55,000	– too early	
Maricult Flotation Ltd	7,000 (+40,000 loan and grant)	22	25,500	– too early	
Shetland-Norse Ltd	4,000 (+30,000 grants)	16	44,700	– too early	
Thaneway Ltd	15,000 (+70,400 loan and grant)	15	99,000	– too early	

Northern Ireland Finance Corporation	Local and regional authority shareholding		Pre-tax profit
	amount £	proportion %	
Andus Electronics (UK) Ltd	90,000 (+270,000 preference shares and loan)	40	
Ards Holdings Ltd	42,000 (+87,500 loan)	28	
Ben Sherman Group	2 (+3,705,914 loan to subsids.)	100	Ceased to trade following sale of certain assets to Department of Commerce

TABLE 4.4 (continued)

Northern Ireland Finance Corporation	Local and Regional Authority Shareholding		Pre-tax profit
	amount £	proportion	
Colin J. Brook & Co. Ltd	6585 pref. (+28,750 shares)	33·3	
Crawford Textiles Ltd	400 pref. (+10,000 shares)	40	
C. Walker and Sons Ltd	13,332 (+1m loan)	49·9	
Fonnom Ltd	2 (+296,926 loan)	100	In receivership
G. H. Patents Ltd	11,400 (+37,500 loan)	100	
Glen Electric Co. Ltd	10,000 (+160,000 loan)	66·67	
John Cleland & Son Ltd	15,000 (+85,000 loan)	25	
Northern Ireland Leather Co. Ltd	100	100	
Oakland Foods Ltd	123,000 (+299,000 loan)	80·4	
Princes Development Co. Ltd	60,000	75	
	(+56,000 loan)		
Regal Styles Ltd	15,000	30·5	In liquidation
Regna International Ltd	500,000 (+1,100,000 loan)	100	In receivership
Strathearn Audio Ltd	4 millions	100	
United Chrometanners Ltd	150,000 (+610,000 loan)	44·8	In liquidation

N.B.: Profit and loss accounts and balance sheets do not have to be made available to the public by Northern Ireland registered companies where there are fewer than 50 members. This means that there is limited information on private capital employed, no information on profits or returns.

Explanatory Notes to Table:

Return on capital employed is a measure of the companies' success as an investment medium: the profits for year X are related to the previous year's capital available, i.e. the position when trading year X began. Profits are shown before interest and tax because it is important to know what the capital employed alone is producing. A return on capital of 10 per cent is an indication that investors have a reasonable expectation of a return of 10 per cent on their money.

There are many different ways of measuring return on capital, depending on the purpose of the exercise. (See *Economic Trends* (November 1974) and *Trade and Industry* (24 October 1975). We have used as a measure of profit what would elsewhere be described as net trading income before interest at historic costs. Our measure of capital employed is net trading assets at historic costs *including* bank loans but excluding overdrafts.

profitability was smaller amongst large firms. From a sample of 15 the annual return during the period September 1974 to October 1976 varied between 14·6 per cent for Rowton Hotels and 0·1 per cent for Adda International, with two firms registering a nil return and a median of 4·2 per cent.[6] In the case of the HIDB firms, Manor Hotel recorded a nil return while Shetland Hotels recorded a return of 8 per cent in the latest figures available before it was taken over in 1973.

In the engineering industry the range of profitability between March 1975 and September 1976 was wide amongst large firms, though the general level was high. From a sample of 15 firms the rate of return varied between 36·1 per cent for Hunt and Moscropt (Middleton) and 14·2 per cent for Ransome Hoffman Pollard, with a median of 22·9 per cent[7] which was considered higher than 'generally associated with makers of capital goods'.[8] Even against this, however, Hi-Fab's return for 1974 of 27 per cent appears very favourable. It is interesting to note that the large firm, George Wimpey, which took over Hi-Fab in 1974 recorded a return for the year ending December 1976 of 18·0 per cent.

The success rate of the HIDB companies as a whole, as far as it is possible to judge, compared favourably with that of private companies unsupported by the state. Between 1968 and 1975 three companies in which the HIDB had shares were liquidated and four were taken over. Excluding those that were liquidated, the profits record for those for which figures are available show a reasonable achievement, and in three cases show a very high achievement. The profits for some other companies were assumed to take longer to secure because a quick return was not expected in the same way as in private commercial investment, and this is often the reason for state intervention in a firm with good, but relatively slow, growth prospects, such as in fish-farming. This record also demonstrates the ability of state shareholding to attract private capital investment into firms which otherwise would not have been able to. There is, of course, another aspect attached to this 'success', in that growth and profitability often lead to takeover, as we have indicated.

For the NIFC or NIDA investment it has not been possible to calculate a rate of return on capital for the companies because insufficient company information has been made publicly available due to different Companies Act requirements in Northern Ireland. Out of 17 companies, four are in liquidation or receivership and one has ceased to trade following the sale of certain of its assets to the Department of Commerce.

Before the NIDA was set up, the NIFC was in some cases willing to invest in rescue or survival cases with an assumed long-term expectation of profitability. Ben Sherman is an example of this type of case. However, regular losses made on firms of this kind led to a change in overall policy by the NIFC because, while it was willing to wait longer than the private sector by itself for a return to be made, this was not intended to be an indefinite period. On the NIFC's recommendation, the NIDA has since dealt with these cases only on a 'directive' from the Department of Commerce where pressure has been put on it to do so from the local area because of excessively high levels of unemployment created by the crisis. While the NIDA always considered the number of jobs involved when assessing what profitability should be expected from an investment, commercial criteria were always applied. Without a 'directive' no jobs would be saved over and above those which were needed during this process. In other words, the basic functioning of a company was on strictly commercial lines. Where assistance was given for expansion purposes, the NIFC or NIDA expected to sell their shares at a capital gain once the reason for their assistance had disappeared, unless they wished to influence the further development of an industry. Where the NIFC and NIDA owned companies they had no active policy to sell or retain their shares. In these cases they preferred, as has been mentioned already, to find a partner to share the risk with them and eventually to sell out completely to the partner.

The rates of return for companies in which local authorities have invested are only available in some cases. Of these, the most spectacular profits have been made by Horizon Midlands. However, figures for this firm must be treated with some caution because the nature of the industry means the rate of return is likely to vary widely from year to year. Horizon Midlands has almost no fixed assets and is dependent on a widely fluctuating demand for its product. For 1975 and 1976 profits were high, reaching a peak for the year ending November 1976 at 91·7 per cent, but 'the market for tours is now thought to have fallen by 15–20 per cent',[9] so that lower profits must be expected in future.

In Blackburn Rovers and Shetland-Norse the companies began to recover after the state intervened. Although they continued to make an overall loss after the state acquired equity, they made large trading profits which, if continued, would eventually eliminate the accumulated losses of previous years. In the London Transport company and in Shetland Aggregates it was too early to assess profitability. Hanson Coach Services made a loss, as it had done before state intervention, while Booth & Fisher made a profit. The intention of the authorities concerned is that all these companies will make profits and not be subsidised.

We have argued that the state is in no way concerned to intervene with equity to assist 'lame ducks'. Exceptions have been made where a firm is allowed to continue without the prospect of profitability only in Northern Ireland and in these cases NIDA has not subsidised the firm's losses. It is concerned to cover its costs and if possible make a profit. During the present period of public expenditure restraint, the purpose of shareholding is to achieve viability of firms with as little cost to the state as possible. Since the NIFC/NIDA does not give grants but only gives loans and equity, it can achieve this objective, covering its own costs over a long period through the repayment of loans and through dividends and capital gains on the sale of shares. The HIDB gives grants as well as loans and equity because it has a wider remit than the NIFC/NIDA, and for this reason it has never expected to cover the cost of its investment. While grants will continue to be given for certain projects in future, they are increasingly being replaced by equity where companies are concerned.

The record of profitability in companies through shareholding by the HIDB, the NIFC/NIDA and local authorities has demonstrated clearly the existence of a capital gap in the finances available to small firms, particularly those involved in manufacturing and commerce. The capital gap is expected to widen as the national economic crisis worsens, creating higher interest rates on borrowed capital, inflation in the cost of machinery and raw or semi-finished materials and in transport costs, and a decrease in the pool of venture capital available.

Shareholding allows the company to continue operating within the market and therefore its commercial objectives remain of paramount importance, wherever the company is located. The equity holding allows the state to protect its investment without assuming the role of day-to-day management of the company's affairs. Once equity has been acquired, continuing contact between the state and the company takes place. The monitoring procedure set up in each case enables the state to inject additional capital or provide other services whenever this is needed to achieve profitability. The limited liability status of the company helps the state to achieve its objective of profitability; it permits the company to operate with the minimum of interference from the state; it enables the state to assist in the restructuring and regeneration of a firm within the process of accumulation; and it means that small amounts of public capital can extract much larger amounts of private capital. Where the state invests, profitability is measured in the same way as where the private sector invests. The exception is that the state will provide financial support where the private sector by itself would not, because the state is prepared to wait longer for a return on capital. But if a company in which the state has invested cannot achieve profitability, then it will be allowed to go into liquidation and the loss of state-owned equity will be accepted on the assumption that most investments will be profitable.

5 Land Development and Infrastructure

In this chapter we discuss the detailed aspects of state shareholding for land development and infrastructure purposes. Schemes involving land development and infrastructure provision are similar in that on the whole they involve the state in facilitating certain kinds of development and protecting the local economy against some of the affects of development.

I FACILITATION, INFLUENCE AND CONTROL

In each case, shareholding evolved as the most appropriate form of intervention to achieve the local authority's planning objectives because it was considered to have certain advantages not possessed by other forms. By examining the alternatives considered by the local authorities, the disadvantages of other methods for achieving the same planning objectives can clearly be seen. In some cases a number of options were available, particularly where the local authority wanted to facilitate a development. In other cases, where control over developments was more important, sometimes the only other option besides shareholding was to operate normal planning procedures by giving planning permissions with conditions attached to them. In yet other cases, there were no alternatives to shareholding at all.

The authorities which formed companies to facilitate development – Manchester, Brighton, Birmingham and Norwich – considered first whether or not a private developer could undertake the work in a way which would achieve their planning objectives. This option was only possible, of course, where the site was already attractive for development, as in Manchester and Birmingham. In these authorities it would have freed the Councils from most of the responsibility of development and, depending on the form of partnership adopted, would have provided them with a quick return on capital from the sale of land and a regular income from rents. Where a site was attractive for a use which did not conform to local planning objectives it might have lain derelict for a long period if left to the private sector to develop.

In Manchester the city centre redevelopment could have been undertaken by a private developer raising the whole of the finance only if the

Council had settled for a smaller site and risked the rest of the site remaining undeveloped for a long time, or if the Council had guaranteed the repayments of loans from financial institutions. The Council was unwilling to guarantee loans because the rate of interest charged by a lending institution would have been higher than that for finance raised directly by the Council. In Birmingham developers could easily have been found to build the national exhibition centre. But the Council wanted to be sure that the project was completed on time and to be involved in the running of such an important local initiative, so it wished to retain some control over its development and operation.

The option of achieving a development through municipal enterprise was considered only by Norwich. It would have provided the authority with complete control over the development together with all the profits from the scheme. Norwich discarded the option to do the building itself on the grounds that the authority could not have financed such a development within the existing constraints on public expenditure.

Partnership arrangements were a more usual option for facilitating development, and had been used extensively during the property boom of the late 1960s and early 1970s, and many were successful; some helped to spread the financial risk between the private sector and local authority, some gave the local authority a chance to alter the terms of an agreement at certain points during the life of the agreement, and some gave significant returns to the public sector. However, traditional partnerships possess major weaknesses which are overcome by shareholding. They are defined by the law of contract and take the form of an agreement which is legally binding and which sets out the terms of the agreement for all time. There may be clauses permitting some revision of terms during the period of the agreement, but there is far more rigidity in the relationship between the local authority and private sector than exists in a shareholding scheme. Therefore in periods of inflation and unstable market conditions these partnership schemes can be unsuitable. The rigidity in the terms of an agreement means that the local authority cannot exert a continuing influence over the development process. In the middle of a development, authorities are often informed that it is no longer feasible for the company to uphold the terms of the partnership. If the scheme is to be completed the authority usually has to accept new terms. But if the authority had been continuously involved in the scheme different solutions to problems might have been found.

Norwich considered using a leasehold arrangement with a developer. This would have enabled the Council to benefit from the increasing value of the development and to gain some control over the development through provisions in a building agreement as ground landlord and lessor as well as planning authority. Also, the developer could have been granted a peppercorn rent until the project was sufficiently completed to yield returns, and, finally, the land would have reverted to the Council at the end of the lease. But the major disadvantages to this type of scheme were that no capital receipt would have accrued to the Council for the value of the land, and the provisions of the 1967 Leasehold Reform Act meant that part of the development would have come within the provisions of the Act; where houses are concerned, and where a lease is over twenty-one years in duration, the leaseholder would be able to enfranchise after five years of occupation and so obtain the freehold.

As with the facilitation of development schemes, companies evolved in order to provide infrastructure or control over public expenditure on infrastructure. Buckingham, Southend, Shetland and the PTEs first considered whether they could achieve their planning objectives by municipalisation, by putting minimal controls on the private sector, or by a traditional partnership agreement with the private sector. In the case of Buckingham, the sites where development was proposed were potentially attractive to private developers once the land had been assembled from the landowners and provided with infrastructure. The local authority was confident there would be no shortage of interest in the sites by private developers once a sewage works had been built to service the area. This was during the 'property boom', when it was assumed the population was rising rapidly in South-East England and the demand for private housing was high. All the local authority had to do was create the conditions for development to occur by making the sites attractive enough to compete favourably with other sites in the area and to achieve this at a low cost to the local authority.

The main problem was to find a method of financing the costs of the infrastructure early on and without the costs falling too heavily on the rates. The local authority considered whether to undertake the scheme as a municipal enterprise. The use of Comprehensive Development Area powers would have allowed the local authority to compulsorily acquire land and provide it with infrastructure. But CDA powers were not suitable because, although they gave the Council control over the management of the development, they did not help to raise finance. In any case, the Council was Conservative-controlled and politically opposed to the use of these powers. Instead the Land Commission's powers were closely examined, but the need to provide infrastructure early on in the scheme meant that they too were unsuitable. The Land Commission would have bought the land, financed the sewage works out of the 40 per cent development gains tax on land sales, and then sold the land on a phased basis. But the capital for the sewage works was needed early and the land sales were unlikely to be achieved quickly enough to recoup the tax necessary to provide it. Negotiations were still in progress with the Commission when a Conservative Government replaced the Labour Government in 1970 and the Land Commission was abolished.

As another alternative, the Council considered a way in which a private developer might assemble and service the sites. The Council approached some big developers with the idea of arranging a joint scheme between the developers and the two Councils involved whereby the developers paid for the sewage works in exchange for the granting of planning permission by the local authority. However, no developers were interested since there were many more attractive sites in the area where planning permissions could be obtained without such a high capital outlay. In any case this option may not have proved acceptable to the Council, since it was regarded as the bartering of a planning permission.

A partnership arrangement was also considered whereby the two Councils, together with developers, would have jointly paid for the infrastructure. But while costs to the Council would have been reduced, the Council would still need to have found a large capital sum and to obtain income from the scheme on a regular basis in order to pay off its debts from the development. This meant that phased payments from phased developments would be needed, which such a joint scheme would not provide. In addition, any normal partnership such as this was risky because it would be difficult to enforce development agreements over, for instance, the allocation and sale of land for particular types of development. Finally, the multiple ownership of land could have led to difficulties in land assembly due to the depressed price of the land on the sites in question.

Besides funding the finance for the sewage works, the Council also wanted to find a method of facilitating development which also gave it some control over the development process. For this reason it rejected using the expanding town provisions of the Town Development Act of 1952. Under the provisions of this Act another Council would have managed the development so that the costs to the Council would have been minimal. But the arrangement would have given too much control to the other Council involved, for instance over housing allocation policy.

In Shetland, the sites proposed for the development of the oil terminal and construction workers' camp were extremely attractive to private investors. However, it was felt that normal controls over development through planning conditions were not adequate to ensure that the planning objectives would be achieved and that a different type of control was needed because the bringing of oil ashore was a major operation and the scale of it could not be estimated with any accuracy. Normal controls were one-off in nature and unsuited to the development of an entirely new and experimental camp; the Council wanted to monitor closely the way the camp was run. Also, the local authority needed to control the developments in such a way as to reduce the possibilities of any adverse effects they might have on the local area, and to reduce the need for unnecessary public expenditure which the developments might create if allowed to go ahead in an uncoordinated way.

In contrast Aberdeen and Peterhead Councils used normal planning controls for providing accommodation for oil-related workers but great

difficulties were encountered in putting large housing programmes with
related services into operation quickly, in suitable locations, and during a
period of local government reorganisation. The local authorities concerned were unused to planning for growth and lacked the staff and
expertise necessary to deal with the pressures on them to accommodate the
influx of population in the region. Delays in construction created heavy
pressure on land in Aberdeen, as a result of which both land and house
prices rose rapidly, seriously limiting the availability of houses for the local
population as well as for incoming workers. Eventually pre-fabricated
houses were assembled rapidly, but they had to be imported from Norway
since there were no available supplies in Britain. The delays in construction therefore not only affected the cost of living for the population in
the area, but adversely affected the balance of payments.[1] At Nigg Bay the
lack of accommodation for oil-related workers became so acute that
Highland Fabricators, the company building the oil platforms in the bay,
bought two liners and moored them in the bay to house the construction
workers temporarily. But this led to a lot of public criticism about the
overcrowding and unhealthy living conditions on the liners.[2] Elsewhere
'caravans multiplied all over the countryside, some of them parked by
arrangement with farmers, others on waste land'.[3]

The situation in Southend was similar to that in Shetland. Again the
Council was concerned to monitor the developments which were to
accompany a major building operation, in this case the third London
airport. As with Shetland, the scale of development was likely to be
substantial and unpredictable in scale especially in the effects it might have
on the local economy and on public infrastructure costs. Normal planning
controls were not sufficient to provide the continuous involvement
required in the planning stages.

Against these alternatives, the advantages gained from company
formation in development were substantial. In some cases the amount of
capital invested by the local authority in shares was very small. While 50 –
100 per cent of the share capital was held in most cases, this amounted to
only £50 in the cases of (SVA) Shetland, Buckingham and Norwich
(Colegate companies), and £100 in Norwich (Conesford). The largest
amount of share capital was held by Manchester at £1,500,000. Through
these shareholdings the local authorities had power to attract a larger
amount of private capital (shares and loans), where this was necessary, and
in different degrees had control over the companies' operations. The
liability of the local authority as shareholder was limited to the amount of
share capital held.

The company form was chosen by Norwich out of five alternatives as the
one that provided the Council with the most benefit and the fewest
significant disadvantages. The establishment of a new company jointly
with a private developer gave the Council the ability to maintain control
over the timing and form of development, and finance for the scheme could

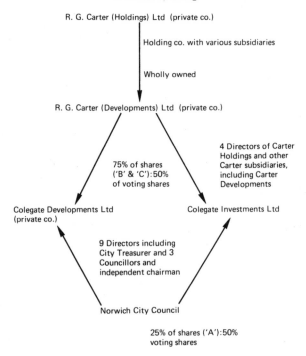

FIGURE 6   Colegate Developments Ltd; Colegate Investments Ltd

1 Holders of 'A' shares have first claim on assets: 'B' and 'C' shares receive dividends: there are 50 'C' shares, and 25 'A' and 25 'B' shares. 'C' shares have no votes. 'A' shares are held by the 4 'A' directors nominated by the council, 'B' shares by the 4 directors nominated by Carters. The 'C' shares are held by Carter (Holdings).

2 Colegate Developments is concerned with residential trading and Colegate Investments with commercial land. The enterprise at Colegate was split into two companies because the Investment activities were a more long-term proposition.

be raised by the company without the Council requiring loan sanction. In addition, the Council could participate in the profits from the scheme, and could recoup the costs of land acquisition more quickly than under other arrangements. Against these advantages it was anticipated that the documentation and legal procedures might be lengthy and complicated, that there would be taxation problems, and that initial legal and advisory costs could be relatively high. However, in the event these problems were not serious.

The original development scheme made provision for forty Flemish-style dwellings at an estimated average price of £21,000 each, a leisure centre, and some commercial space in listed historic buildings. In order to deal with this, two separate companies were formed, Colegate Developments Ltd and Colegate Investments Ltd, in which the Council owned 25 per cent of the total shares and 50 per cent of the voting shares, and in each of which the Council and Carter (the private developer) had four directors with an independent chairman. The Council was to receive 70 per cent of the Development company profits and 50 per cent of the Investment company profits. The financial relationship between the two companies was complex. Some Development company profits were intended to be loaned to the Investment company to cover all or some of its land costs. The Investment company's overdraft was therefore intended to be short-term and dependent upon the success of the Development company. It was always envisaged that the Investment activities were more of a more long-term kind and this arrangement would have reduced that company's debt burden considerably.

During the development process a large number of external factors affected the performance of these companies and led to a number of revisions to the scheme. These would not have been possible had a traditional partnership been used. Firstly, the scheme was delayed by labour and material shortages and large cost increases caused by the shortage of materials. Adjustments to the scheme were made so that the development as a whole would remain viable. Secondly, part of the site originally intended for the leisure centre subsequently became listed buildings. This made the leisure centre idea questionable because of the reduction in available land. A revised scheme for the remainder of what was to have been the leisure centre site provided for an office block, a pub and a restaurant. The listed buildings on the rest of the leisure centre site were to be converted into flats and offices. Later on the economic situation worsened and more adjustments had to be made. It became impracticable to proceed with the original intention that the Council should lease the site of the intended office block, pub and restaurant to the Investment company, which would then have constructed the buildings and sub-leased them at a premium. This part of the total project was, therefore, postponed. By 1977 it was envisaged that the Investment company would be making profits in ten years' time. The Development company had ended up making a small loss overall. As a result, it could not pay off the Investment company's overdraft and a further loan had to be raised for the Investment company which the council and Carters jointly guaranteed. In view of the collapse of the property market since 1972, when the scheme was set up, the Council regarded the scheme as a success, achieving aims which the private market, left to itself, could not have achieved.

When the Council decided that a second company was needed to develop a small site within a large development area they chose to form a wholly-owned company, Conesford Ltd. This had three advantages over and above the joint scheme with Carters. Firstly, the Council would

FIGURE 7 Conesford Development Co. Ltd

receive all the development profits (but no builders' profits), thereby benefiting from any upswing in the market; it would also sustain all the losses, of course, should the market collapse. Secondly, it would obtain complete control over the selection and implementation of schemes which would avoid the problem of developers reneging on partnership arrangements, and would eliminate the need to negotiate any changes in a scheme with a partner. Finally, 100 per cent Council ownership rather than 50 per cent ownership in partnership with another company meant that the Council's interest could not be affected by any financial or management problems experienced by the partner's company. This was something which had at one stage worried the Council in the Colegate scheme.

In Buckingham a company was formed in conjunction with an option agreement to facilitate the development of particular sites. Together these gave maximum flexibility to the Councils over land assembly and sale for development. Under this scheme, the Council would share the development gains with the landowners, and the profit from the company could be used for facilities in the town; for sharing of profits with landowners would provide a catalyst for the landowners to sell when the value of their land was depressed, and finally, the risk on the land acquisition and infrastruc-

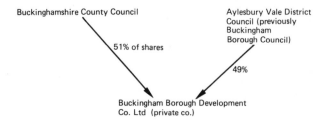

FIGURE 8   Buckingham Borough Development Co. Ltd

ture development would be spread between the landowners and the company.

As in Norwich, the company provided Buckingham Borough Council with continuous control over the scheme where changes in market conditions meant that adaptations were needed. The Council's 100 per cent ownership of the company meant it was easy to adapt the scheme to avoid any losses being made. The original scheme was modified soon after it was started in response to a very different economic climate and a slower projected population growth in South-East England. Two major changes were made to the original scheme which both involved carrying losses or costs for longer than at first envisaged. Firstly, in 1976 the drainage agreement was renegotiated and a new completion date and arrangement for repayment of sewage costs were agreed. Land sales were slower than originally expected, so the repayment was extended from 1978 to 1983, and the company no longer had to pay the full costs of the sewage works. The company agreed to pay £150 per dwelling (which was less than the full sewage costs per house), with a block sum being paid for all the dwellings planned to be erected on land already sold. In respect of future land sales, the payment of £150 would be made as each house was sold by the developer.

Secondly, in 1977 the company considered the possibility of developing one of the housing areas by a form of partnership with a developer. The arrangement proposed was to provide the developer with a licence to build dwellings without any initial payment for the land. On completion of each dwelling the freehold interest would be passed directly from the company to the house purchaser and at that time the developer would be responsible for paying the company 10 per cent of the sale price of the house. The agreement included conditions whereby the developer was responsible for developing approximately 50 per cent of the housing area at a certain rate of dwellings per annum. The agreement also allowed the developer to extend the development to the second part of the housing area subject to renegotiation regarding the percentage payment to be paid to the company. The ring road in the housing area would be financed by the company and constructed by the County Council. A small area of land within the area was temporarily reserved for local authority housing.

The Sullom Voe Association in Shetland is an example of a company formed mainly for control purposes, in this case for control over oil terminal developments. A partnership between the Council and oil companies was formed as a joint company which owned no assets and was non-profit-making. It contained two Council directors and two oil company directors. Its purpose was to 'control, supervise and generally organise the design, construction, operation, management and mainten-ance of the terminal'. Sullom Voe Association Ltd (SVA) also had two advisory groups: the Technical Working Group, which included oil industry technical staff and Council representatives, considered detailed

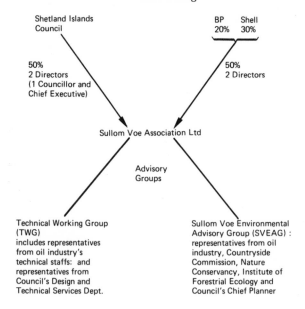

Shetland Islands
Council

BP   Shell
20%   30%

50%
2 Directors
(1 Councillor and
Chief Executive)

50%
2 Directors

Sullom Voe Association Ltd

Advisory
Groups

Technical Working Group
(TWG)
includes representatives
from oil industry's
technical staffs: and
representatives from
Council's Design and
Technical Services Dept.

Sullom Voe Environmental
Advisory Group (SVEAG) :
representatives from oil
industry, Countryside
Commission, Nature
Conservancy, Institute of
Forestrial Ecology and
Council's Chief Planner

FIGURE 9   Sullom Voe Association Ltd

1 BP and Shell are pipeline operators for the Ninian and Brent fields respectively.
2 SVEAG advises on matters affecting the environment. TWG considers detailed
  technical points.
3 Three observers attend SVA meetings, one from Chevron (Ninian field), one
  from Esso (Brent field) and one from Conoco (which represents the Oil Liaison
  Committee – a committee of *all* the companies with finds in the Shetland area,
  i.e. not jut the major pipeline operators).

technical points and reports to the SVA; the Sullom Voe Environmental
Advisory Group (SVEAG) included representatives from the oil industry,
conservancy groups and the Council, and gave advice on environmental
matters.

The SVA and SVEAG were involved in a major dispute over
underground storage prior to the submission of the application by the oil
industry to develop the terminal at Sullom Voe. The Council's case was
that underground storage was a better safeguard against pollution and
sabotage than surface storage. The Council added that it was also going to
be virtually impossible to reinstate the site after usage if surface tanks were
used because of the massive gorges into hillsides which have to be made to
provide level surfaces. The Council argued that the oil industry had not
shown that underground storage was prohibitively expensive or technically unusable. The oil industry disputed this and put the cost at over

£30m; it also foresaw technical difficulties increasing the cost further and disagreed with the Council that the rock structure was suitable for underground storage.

The oil industry representatives on the SVA forced a vote on the issue and the Council representatives 'deplored the pressure being exerted by the oil industry to force an unconsidered decision'.[4] The voting was deadlocked since neither side had a majority of directors or shares. The matter was formally reported by the Council representatives on SVA to the Council. The Convenor's report commented on the 'stubbornness of the industry's representatives' which

> puts them in a situation which could result in many months, if not years, of delay. Whether or not this was their intention I have to report to you that your representatives are acting in a way which is consistent with your past approach and are approaching the matter in a constructive way. While they refuse to be harassed they will do all in their power to ensure that the matter is dealt with expeditiously. Naturally, you will be kept advised of developments as they take place.[5]

Soon after this the Council withdrew from the SVEAG. The Council argued that the chairman and secretary of the Group, both BP representatives, should be replaced by independent people. The SVEAG was alleged to be insufficiently impartial to give the SIC the advice it needed. It was known at the time that the forthcoming report of the SVEAG on the environmental impact of the oil developments was equivocal on the cavern storage issue.[6] Later, the chairman and secretary did resign so that SVEAG could elect new officers independent of the SIC and the oil industry. However, SVEAG was meanwhile virtually at a standstill without SIC representatives.

By the middle of the following month the SIC agreed by 13 votes to 3 to climb down on the cavern storage issue. The SIC expected the oil industry in return to accept proposals for joint treatment facilities for the oil, rather than a proliferation of facilities for each company. This was eventually agreed to. By December 1976 there were also proposals for a new SVEAG put forward by the Council which included provisions for independent conflict resolution.

In the case of the joint company formed by the SIC and Bateman Catering Ltd to operate the construction workers' camp, the Council had a majority of shares (by one) and appointed 3 out of the 6 directors. In January 1976 the catering workers at the camp went on strike over pay and conditions. This meant that construction workers who lived in the camp had to be flown out of Shetland. Work on the oil terminal stopped. The dispute was handled mainly by Batemans. The chief executive of the Council, one of the company's directors, announced that the Council would not be able to accept the catering workers' demands for a pay increase which would breach the national £6 pay policy. Eventually the

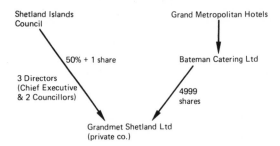

FIGURE 10   Grandmet Shetland Ltd

1 Share capital 10,000: council's share capital given by partners

dispute was settled by Batemans in March by various extra allowances being given to the catering workers to settle their demands. The Council played a minimal role in the settlement.

Shortly after this another issue arose. Shetlanders working on the construction site pressed the Council to be allowed to live in the camp. The Council had originally opposed this because it feared that labour would flock from remote areas of the Shetland Isles and from the Council's own workforce in order to work on the site and live in the camp. BP was also unwilling to allow workers with a Shetland home address to live there because it argued that the expensive camp (it cost £100 a week to keep each construction worker there) had been constructed especially to house non-Shetlanders and to minimise the burden on facilities and services for Shetlanders. Under pressure from Councillors the Council changed its mind, but the decision could have little affect on BP's policy since BP was the tenant of the camp. A letter from the Firth camp manager to one of the Council's directors on Grandmet as late as October 1976 stated that no decision had been communicated to him about a change in policy towards Shetlanders.

There was therefore a great deal of uncertainty about the Council's role in relation to the camp. By 1977 the Council directors began to enquire into various aspects of camp policy. It was also agreed by the Council that the Council's Environmental Health and Control Committee would maintain a review of the life of the camp. The Council did manage to influence the purchasing policy of the company so that a Shetland concern provided the camp with supplies. But the main point is that the original reason for state control of the company had evaporated, leaving the Council in a position where other management issues were relatively unimportant. The arrival of 1100 construction workers in Shetland did not give rise to the various problems the Council feared. There was therefore little reason for further intervention. When a second camp was built nearby at Toft the Council did not repeat the joint company idea but settled for imposing extensive planning conditions, one of which was that a monitoring group be set up between the Council and the oil industry 'to assess and continually review the impact of oil-related projects, including the Toft construction village, on local labour patterns'.

Shetland Towage did not begin to operate fully until 1977. The Council's Ports and Harbours Committee was involved in extensive negotiations with the oil companies over the number of tugs and other facilities which would be provided. The more elaborate the safety provisions, the higher the cost to the oil companies for using the tuggage facilities. The Council argued that when the tugs were fully operational the joint company should provide the Council with continuous control over the operation of facilities and the maintenance of safety and anti-pollution measures. The Council considered that without its participation in the company, the oil companies might come to some operating arrangement with a private shipping company which would not maximise safety features.

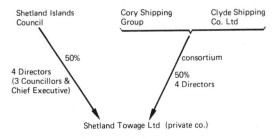

FIGURE 11   Shetland Towage Ltd

1 Share capital of £200,000 (+£1m. non-voting shares): £50,000 of council's £100,000 given free by partners.

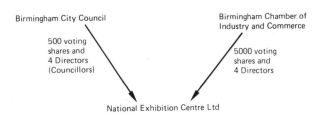

FIGURE 12   National Exhibition Centre Ltd

The main advantage of Birmingham's shareholding in the National Exhibition Centre Ltd was that it combined local authority control with the commercial freedom of action of a company. There was a fail-safe clause in the Articles of Association which gave the Council a casting vote in the event of deadlock on the company's board. Control could have been achieved in other ways, for instance through a joint committee of the Council and Chamber of Industry and Commerce, over which the Council had ultimate control. However, the joint ownership of a company with the Chamber meant that the operations of the company could also take place outside the relatively time-consuming Council-committee cycles and interdepartmental consultative working parties; it enabled separate and speedier, more *ad hoc* industrial relations and disputes arrangements to be evolved in order to complete the scheme on time.

In Buckingham, Birmingham, Norwich and Shetland control over a company's operations required them to hold at least 50 per cent of the voting shares and to have at least half of the directors on the board. This was not necessary in the case of Southend however, where only 18 per cent of the shares were held by the Council in the Thames Estuary Development Company Ltd. This was because the Council was not so concerned with managing the development to the same extent as the other local authorities we have discussed; it wanted to support the idea of reclaiming Foulness for the airport, and wanted to be able to influence any proposals for development at Foulness in a positive way as a shareholder and board member when introducing local land-use planning considerations into the decision-making. While the Council's shareholding was small, no other shareholder held more than 18 per cent in the consortium.

In the cases of Manchester and Brighton, the Councils were mainly concerned to raise finance through a company in which they owned shares

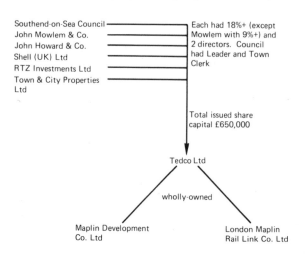

FIGURE 13 Thames Estuary Development Co. Ltd

for the construction of a city centre scheme and a conference centre respectively. The Brighton Civic Development Company Ltd was formed with Councillors as shareholders and directors, and a building agreement was shared by the Council, Longleys (the developer) and the company. The Council managed to facilitate a scheme in accordance with its planning objective, which did not impose a large burden on public expenditure. Also, it gave the local authority power to control the initial funding arrangements through its Councillor/director shareholders, and enabled them to raise finance from Guinness Mahon, through the company, to be paid back over a period of thirty of years under a deferred-purchase arrangement.

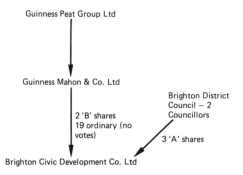

FIGURE 14   Brighton Civic Development Co. Ltd

Companies were used in Manchester in a similar fashion to raise finance, because the Prudential was unwilling to finance the whole cost of a development; but in this case the Council held a substantial shareholding in the Manchester Mortgage Corporation and Second Manchester Mortgage Corporation. The particular advantages of the Council-owned companies in this case were that money could be raised at a lower rate of interest with the Council's backing; it could be raised without having to affect the Council's financial allocation from central government. The raising of money would not be a contravention of central government restrictions (Circular 2/70) since the money was being raised for use in the private, not the public, sector; also, the money would be secured on the developers' (Town & City) assets and properties elsewhere. Additional advantages were that the Council's involvement in raising finance meant the whole site became attractive for development, and the Corporation could share in the profits of the development. Against all these advantages, the Council had to guarantee the money, and as a large sum had to be raised, some of it on the stock market, the Council had to acquire a substantial company in order to do this. However, the end result was that it was able to share the risks of development with the other financial

Manchester Corporation

wholly owned

7 Directors
(Councillors)

Manchester Mortgage Corporation Ltd

wholly owned

Second Manchester Mortgage Corporation Ltd

FIGURE 15   Manchester Mortgage Corporation Ltd

institution involved throughout the development scheme, enabling the
scheme to be completed when the market was unable to take the full risk
itself.

The reasons why Passenger Transport Executives formed companies
were also largely financial. The Merseyside, West Midlands and Tyne and
Wear PTEs' group relief schemes helped to reduce the costs to the PTEs of
providing transport services in their area during a period of public
expenditure restraint. PTEs also bought shares in companies for other
reasons where no other arrangement would have offered the same
advantages. For example, in order to retain the service conditions
structure for the staff and the continuous operation of the newly acquired
Midland Red service, the establishment of West Midlands Passenger
Transport Ltd avoided the costly retraining of new staff and any break in
transport services.

Local authority shareholding facilitates development or infrastructure
provision without incurring increases in state expenditure. It gives a
greater degree of continuous control or influence than other forms of
intervention in the particular overall economic context we have been
considering. All the other alternative forms of intervention we have
described were inappropriate in one way or another; municipalisation,
traditional partnerships (subject to law of contract rather than company
law) and planning controls, did not give the advantages of limited liability,
or of raising private finance by the state sharing in the risk, or of continuous
monitoring and control, or of a share in the return.

Shareholding for land development and infrastructure should therefore
be seen in terms of its applicability to a number of different circumstances
in the crisis. It facilitates developments, it influences or controls aspects of
developments and it reduces public expenditure and the effects of

development on the local economy. All of these objectives have acquired a particular urgency because of the crisis.

II COMMERCIAL INDEPENDENCE AND PROFITABILITY

Both the state and the private sector involved in the companies aimed at ultimate viability or profitability for the particular kind of development. The Councils' role was therefore not to introduce non-commercial criteria into the enterprise. Controlled facilitation meant making a commercial success of a scheme which the Council wanted to see implemented in a certain way. This was achieved by the Councils retaining substantial influence or control over major policy issues, while day-to-day decisions on the companies' operations were taken by the management of the company.

In the development and infrastructure companies the management of the company involved public authority directors comprising up to half or more of the board. Many of these directors were the chairmen of committees or the chief officers of departments; the Chairman of Housing, Vice-Chairman of Planning in Norwich; the Chairman of the Conference Committee in Brighton; the Chairman of Finance in Buckingham; most key committee Chairmen in Manchester; the Leader of the Council and the Chief Executive in Southend and Shetland; the Director of Finance in the case of some PTE companies. These directors often helped the process of policy control because they led committees or departments which had a particular interest in the companies' activities. However, the key to policy control was the actual reporting back or integration of certain company activities with other Council committee work.

The initial decision of the Council to intervene was always taken by the Council itself, or a Council committee. In all cases, major policy decisions of the companies always came back to the Council or committee where a substantial change in the scheme was necessary, such as an increase in the finance required. Where there was no reporting back, this was usually because there were no major policy issues to take back for decision. Although the companies were free from day-to-day control of their operations, they did not pursue their own objectives as something completely separate from the state. The objectives were pursued with the agreement of, or in accordance with, the policies of the state.

In Norwich the Council appointed four directors to the Colegate Companies. There was also a working party comprising the City Treasurer, the Architect, the Council's Estates Surveyor and the Development Director of Carters, which had delegated powers to make decisions which could not wait for a board meeting. It acted mainly as a forum where details were examined and clarified prior to board meetings. These arrangements aided the smooth running of the management side of the company. The reporting back to Council committees was limited to gaining the approval of financial guarantees which had to be obtained from the Finance Committee, and gaining planning permission for the original and subsequently revised scheme which had to be obtained from the Planning Committee.

In Buckingham there was also a working party of the company called the Land Transactions Committee, which comprised one member from each of the two Councils with shares in the company along with the company's general manager, the County Architect. This committee dealt with the detailed arrangements concerning land sales and purchases. Each large land transaction was then reported to the County Secretary and Solicitor as the County Council was a debenture holder in the company. Again, the company had to have the Finance Committee's approval to borrow money from the Council, and all the housing schemes for which land was assembled and sold to developers had to have outline planning permission from the Planning Committee.

In the Shetland SVA, there was little formal reporting back to the Council by the Council's directors on detailed SVA discussions concerning planning applications and progress in development. But major actions by the Council, such as its position on underground oil storage and withdrawal from the SVEAG, were always based on Council decisions. SVA's responsibility was to discuss and agree, where possible, major applications for planning permission by the oil industry, such as the £300m. storage and process development itself at Sullom Voe. This application involved policy issues, such as underground storage, which had already been resolved by the Council and the oil companies and not just the SVA. In other words, there was very little independent SVA activity over major policy issues, only on details. The Council also proceeded to impose 43 planning conditions on the eventual permission to develop at Sullom Voe. These included 20 'general' conditions, defining the area in which the development could take place, the dumping of peat, supplies of heavy materials, storage and disposal of chemicals and waste, accommodation of the workforce, possible alterations to the plans, safety and security of the terminal. Detailed proposals for the handling of oil spillage had to be submitted to the Council and approved before the terminal started operating. Conditions applied to the tanks were aimed at making them as safe as possible, and the oil industry was obliged to alter the four storage tanks already under construction to include the most recently agreed safety features.[7]

In Birmingham the NEC company was regarded as the management agent for the city. The board of the company reported to an NEC committee of the Council on financial policy and other major policy matters such as a new departure in the construction plans which proposed the building of a workshop and warehousing which the company would manage. The relative independence of the company from the Council's normal operations had a purpose, particularly in the field of labour relations. The centre was built at a time of free collective bargaining when it was relatively easy to settle disputes in an *ad hoc*, one-off manner according to procedures agreed by labour and management. A special procedural agreement was arrived at which helped to resolve disputes on the NEC construction site where several unions were involved. This could not have happened within a local government structure where negotiations would be slower and related more to annual, national negotiations over pay and conditions. In the five years during which the NEC was built only six hours of working time were lost in industrial disputes. After 1975 this record would have been more difficult to achieve because of the deterioration in the economic situation and the implementation of an incomes policy which ended free collective bargaining. The company device and its independence from local government proceedings also meant that part-time female labour from the near-by Chelmsley Wood estate could be employed much more easily on an *ad hoc* basis.

The PTE companies were also integrated into the policy process, while being autonomous so far as day-to-day operations were concerned. The County Councils approved all the decisions concerning the purchase of shares and the raising of finance. Each PTE was also linked very closely to a number of committees of the Council, such as transportation, planning and finance. In the case of the tax relief and capital grants schemes that the PTEs got involved in, there would be no reasons for any further involvement of the Council once the scheme was operational.

It can be seen that the independence of the companies in day-to-day management had advantages in allowing the delegation of detailed policy implementation. This delegation was usually operated within mechanisms of overall policy control. Fundamental agreement between the Councils and the companies about objectives meant that there were no major conflicts between the roles played by the state and the company; these roles involved the control of policy by the Councils on the one hand, and the implementation of policy by the companies on the other.

We must now examine the extent to which the schemes achieved viability or profitability out of this compatibility of roles. Firstly, we should distinguish between the particular scheme or development and the Council company involved in the development. Frequently, the company was only concerned with a part of the development, such as financing in Manchester and Brighton, or land assembly and servicing in Buckingham. The profitability of the company could therefore be different from the profitability of the development as a whole. For instance, the PTE companies and the SVA did not aim to achieve profitability for the company itself. In the Manchester scheme, profits of the company itself were deliberately kept low to avoid payment of corporation tax, while the local authority benefited from the profits of the overall development and from the revenue obtained as freeholder of the land on which the development was taking place. The schemes themselves were on the whole

TABLE 5.1 Local and regional authority shareholding, private capital and financial return (land development and infrastructure)

Local and regional authority	Local and regional authority shareholding amount £	Local and regional authority shareholding proportion %	Private capital (share and loan capital £)	Pre-tax profit (return on capital employed)	Return to the authority
Norwich (Colegate)	50	50	725,000		50% of projected profits of development and leases
(Conesford)	100	100	200,000		All profits
Manchester	1,500,000	100	45 m. for project as a whole	Cover costs plus small profit	25% approx. of projected profits of development (est. £125,000 + per annum) + leases
Brighton	2	40	5·5 m.		Income from conference centre
Birmingham	50,000	50			Estimated profitability of NEC in 1980s: all income to local authority
Southend	118,182	15	530,000		Proportionate share to authority
Shetland (Towage)	100,000	50	1,200,000	'Tens of thousands a year' once fully in operation	
(Grandmet)	5001	50·001	4999		
(SVA)	50	50	300 m. for project as a whole	Not applicable	Receives oil disturbance allowance in proportion to amount of oil brought ashore. Estimated at £40+m for the duration of North Sea oil

Local and regional authority	Local and regional authority shareholding		Private capital (share and loan capital £)	Pre-tax profit (return on capital employed)	Return to the authority
	amount £	proportion			
Buckinghamshire and Aylesbury	50 (+200,000 loan)	100	250,000		25% of projected profit of land sales
Greater Manchester PTE (Lancashire United)	1,404,832	100	185,000	3% (1974)	All profits
(SELNEC Transport Services)	25	100	75	Not applicable because company concerned with group relief	Share in group relief
West Midlands PTE (Pearson Green)	240	100	760	Not applicable – group relief	Share in group relief
(W. Midlands Passenger Transport Ltd)	100	100		not applicable because of operations of company – to maintain service and conditions structure for staff	
Merseyside PTE (Passenger Transport Services Ltd)	24	100	75	Not applicable – group relief	Share in group relief
Tyne & Wear PTE (Transport Services Ltd)	25	100	376	Not applicable – group relief	Share in group relief
All PTEs (Transport Tokens Ltd)	8000	40	Other capital is from other public bodies	2% approx.	To cover costs

meant to achieve profits, either in the form of return on capital for the company, the overall profits of the development, or from group relief. In other words, unlike the manufacturing companies discussed in the previous chapter, *profitability for the company itself* was not an objective in every case: but profitability *for the scheme or development* was.

The amounts of private capital required for the schemes and the companies involved can be seen in Table 5.1. Small amounts of money facilitated or controlled developments involving £ thousands or £ millions. The main objective was to facilitate this investment in a controlled way, and to share in profit-making.

For instance, in the case of the SVA the aim was to facilitate a profitable and very expensive development in a controlled way. Facilitation, in the case of the SVA, meant speeding up a development which was already taking place. It is often thought that the actions of the Shetland Islands Council delayed the oil developments considerably, particularly when the issue of underground storage arose. By 1976 it was estimated that oil was going to be brought ashore two to three years later than was originally envisaged, partly as a result of SIC's stand against the oil companies. But the development of the oil terminal at Sullom Voe faced substantial problems which did not involve the Council. The main difficulty was that there were twenty-eight different oil companies taking part in the negotiations. BP and Shell did most of the bargaining with the Council, but had to obtain agreement from all the other companies. This often incurred difficulties which led to considerable delays over the submission of planning applications.

The role of the SVA was to expedite the planning and implementation process. As with all the other local authority involvement in companies, the objectives of the SIC and the oil companies were far closer than many would expect. The rhetoric surrounding the Shetland case disguises the fact that twenty-eight oil companies eventually agreed to the joint use of processing facilities. Instead of accepting the proliferation of facilities, the Council argued for joint use on the grounds of environmental protection. By so doing, it encouraged a decision which was a cheaper and more efficient solution. It was cheaper and more efficient for the oil companies, the local economy and the state because it saved public expenditure and private capital by forcing the companies to share facilities and infrastructure, it speeded up the process of bringing the oil ashore and processing it, and it avoided the shattering of local fishing grounds by the endless proliferation of pipelines.

The Council achieved these things through the vehicle of the SVA. Its power to take equity was the key to this process since it enabled the oil companies to do something which they would not have done independently, either as individual companies or as a syndicate. An ex-convenor of SIC has written that:

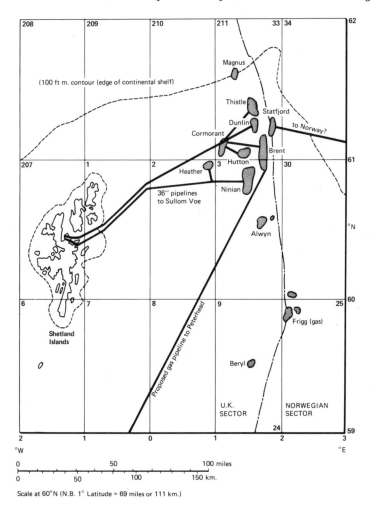

FIGURE 16 Portion of the Shetland Basin oil fields and pipelines in relation to the
Shetland Islands
Reproduced with permission from *Oil Terminal Sullom Voe: Environment Impact
Assessment* (Thuleprint, May 1976)
PARTICIPANTS IN THE NINIAN AND BRENT PIPELINE GROUPS (%)

Ninian Pipeline Group		*Brent Pipeline Group*	
BP Petroleum Development Ltd	13·0	Shell (UK) Ltd	34·2
Ranger Oil (UK) Ltd	5·2	Esso Exploration & Production (UK)	34·2
Scottish Canadian Oil & Transportation Co.Ltd	1·8	Conoco North Sea	3·9
		Gulf Oil Production Co.	3·9

London & Scottish Marine Oil Co. Ltd	4·0	National Coal Board (Exploration) Ltd	3·9
Cawoods Holdings Ltd	1·0	Burmah Oil Developments Ltd	2·2
National Carbonising Co.Ltd	1·0	Sante Fé Minerals (UK)	2·1
Burmah Oil (North Sea) Ltd	18·3	Champlin Petroleum Co. (UK)	2·1
Imperial Chemical Industries Ltd	15·8	United Canso Oil and Gas (UK) Ltd	1·9
Murphy North Sea Co.	6·0	Tricentral North Sea Ltd	0·9
Ocean Overseas Co.	6·0	Charterhouse Securities Ltd	0·1
Chevron Petroleum (UK) Ltd	14·6	Amoco (UK) Exploration Co.	1·4
		Gas Council (Exploration) Ltd	1·4
		Amerada Petroleum Corporation (UK) Ltd	1·0
		North Sea Inc.	0·6
		Mobil North Sea Ltd	1·1
		Texaco North Sea (UK) Co.	5·0
			100·0

Apart from the control and earning power [the provision to take equity] conferred, there is a deeper significance. The existence of this clause and county council [as it was pre-1975] involvement in the operation of Sullom Voe together, have enabled the oil companies to go ahead to their joint-user activities without any fear of the American Anti-Trust laws.[8]

In other words the power of the SIC justified the formation of an operating cartel which could not have happened without the SIC. The operating cartel was not illegal in US law because it was not self-imposed, but it would be extremely profitable to the oil companies concerned.

The Council was aware of the need to operate in the 'national interest' particularly when self-sufficiency in oil production was said to be a significant contribution to alleviating Britain's crisis. The SIC conceded over underground storage because of what it saw to be central government's concern for the 'national interest'. As a result, the argument that Shetland is a unique growth area and therefore a special case loses much of its attraction. In times of crisis, boom areas are driven by the same dynamic that operates in the rest of the country. National level factors make special cases very similar to any other cases. In Shetland the outcome of the SIC's negotiations with the oil companies over the all-important £300m. terminal was to impose extensive controls and also to facilitate an even more profitable development.

In Manchester, Shetland and Buckingham large profits were expected from the developments when completed, and the local authority would receive its share as indicated in Table 5.1. In Birmingham, the company continued to manage the operations of the National Exhibition Centre once it was completed. The break-even point for the centre was estimated at 180 days of bookings per annum. By the end of 1976 it had achieved this and there were over 200 days booked for the forthcoming year. An operating profit for the centre was expected for 1977 and it was estimated that by 1983 the centre would be clearly profitable after taking interest charges into account. The final costs of buildings and financing (including accumulated funding of the company since 1971) were known by the end of 1976. After deducting the £1.5m. government grant, total costs were £38m. repayable over forty years. This was higher than original estimates because of higher building costs and interest rates but did not affect the estimated date of overall profitability.

Not all the development schemes made profits as such. We have already referred to the fact that one of the Norwich companies made a small loss, although profits were expected from the others. Interim losses on the Norwich Colegate companies had been consolidated into Carters accounts, since Carters owned 75 per cent of the share capital (though only 50 per cent of voting shares). Like Whitbreads and Rothschilds in the PTE group relief companies, this enabled Carters to claim tax relief on other operations. In Southend the total accumulated loss of the company by 1973 amounted to £653,000 but this was only £3000 more than the share capital. This reflected the unprofitable research stage of the venture, including the reports to the Roskill Commission on the third London airport and subsequent feasibility studies for the development. The Council felt that the proposals of the Thames Estuary Development Company influenced the Department of the Environment's eventual decision to reject Roskill's recommendation of the Cublington site for the airport, and to select Maplin. British Rail also started to consider a joint venture with the company for building the rail link to London. However, in 1974 the government abandoned the third London airport idea because of the state of the economy. The companies remained in existence. From the Council's point of view they had achieved one of the primary objectives of securing the site for South-East Essex.

In Brighton the company itself was not intended to make profits, but just to raise money for the conference centre scheme. The advantage of the company arrangement was that the Council repaid the loan over thirty years. The financial advantage to the Council was the income from the conference centre. The private sector retained all the profits from the development itself.

The PTE companies concerned with group tax relief also did not make profits as such. They did however produce substantial revenue for the PTEs from group relief. For example, the Greater Manchester company SELNEC Transport Services Ltd received £660,000 in one year – 'an amount receivable from a third party in respect of the surrender of tax losses in accordance with the group relief provisions of the Income and Corporation Taxes Act 1970'; in the same year Tyneside Transport

Services Ltd received £220,000; Merseyside £260,000; Pearson Green Ltd (West Midlands) £372,304. These sums of money were then divided between the PTEs and the large companies involved in the group relief provisions. National Transport Tokens made a small return and in 1975 acquired a 27 per cent stake in The Birmingham Mint Ltd.

Unlike the manufacturing companies, the development and infrastructure companies or projects often produced profits or revenues which were not necessarily reinvested in the same project or company. Many companies were designed for one particular project, and many projects had a fixed termination date not requiring a continuing concern for retained earnings. In the manufacturing companies the state's share of the profits could be used elsewhere but only after the company had retained some of the earnings for its own use. This was to be expected from the different production processes involved. The development projects were spatially discrete products which were only part of the large companies' more extensive activities. With the manufacturing companies the public authorities were involved in the whole production process of a company and with the turnover of capital in the company as a whole. In the case of the development and infrastructure companies this only applied to Lancashire United Transport, National Transport Tokens and the PTE leasing companies which used to be group relief companies; in other words, it only applied to the transport companies. In these companies the state was involved with the whole of the production process and not just a small part of a larger company's concern; there was no foreseeable date when either the company would complete its existing tasks, or the state would be no longer involved; there would also be a reinvestment of some of the profits over a considerable period of time.

Although the development schemes ended at a particular time, revenue or profits would still be obtained from many of them: in Manchester and Norwich in the form of rents, leases and/or a share of the large companies' rent revenue from the completed scheme; in Birmingham and Brighton in the form of income from the specific use of the constructed buildings (exhibition centre and conference centre). There was also a restraint on dividend payment for a period, so the arrangement whereby the local authorities frequently received most of their income from the development scheme outside the mechanisms of company operations worked to their advantage. They also tried to minimise the tax payable on their income from the company, in Norwich's case by treating its profits from the companies as charges against the company (like loan interest) *before* tax was paid. In Manchester the profits from the company were kept very low in order to reduce Corporation Tax to a minimum. In both cases the main profits of the local authorities would come from the development as a whole; in Norwich from the Colegate Investment commercial properties in the form of rents and leases to the council as landowner; and in Manchester from leases and from a share of the Town & City/Prudential profits which was proportionate to the Council's financial contribution to the scheme.

In most cases the local authority had no specific plans for its share of the profits. In Buckingham there was a possibility that they would be spent on some aspects of conservation, or to provide some activity which could not otherwise be provided. In Shetland the profits would be used along with the disturbance allowance and other oil-related income to invest in local industry. Shetland was the only example where income from schemes described in this chapter would be used to invest in companies described in the previous chapter. In the other schemes the local economy was protected more indirectly, through state control of some of the development activity that has been described in this chapter.

In conclusion, the viability of the schemes should be considered not just in terms of the degree of success of the local authority in achieving its 'land-use planning' objectives. The schemes should also be considered in terms of the revenue generated, or the investment facilitated by local authority involvement, and in terms of the profitability of the schemes to private investors and to the state. The state did not achieve company viability or project profitability at its own expense. Planning objectives and company profitability should instead be seen as compatible rather than conflicting.

Part III

Conclusions

6 Shareholding as Managed Intervention

In this final chapter we discuss local and regional authority shareholding in relation to the theoretical apporaches outlined in the Introduction and the implications local and regional shareholding has for the 'planning' system we also outlined in the Introduction.

In previous chapters we have discussed the role of the state in the crisis; we have seen how local and regional authorities have assumed the role of risk-takers through the medium of the limited liability company. The introduction of limited liability in company law over 100 years ago greatly extended the centralisation of capital and expanded the accumulation process. The more systematic use of state shareholding since the mid-1960s at national, regional and local levels has represented a further use of limited liability in the accumulation process. It has enabled the state to encourage investment and development in a controlled way. The limited liability of the shareholder is a basic safeguard for the state in facilitating investment and development in an accumulation crisis where state expenditure in general is strictly controlled. At the same time the involvement of the state in risk-taking attracts private capital, facilitates investment and controls development. The advantage of state shareholding to private capital is in fact its limited nature. The state's support for an investment is limited in its liability to the state and it limits the liability of other investors by sharing in the risk of a particular venture; it is also restricted in its extent and in its duration.

We must now examine this new extension of entrepreneurial activity by the state in relation to some of the functions of the state in capital accumulation. Firstly, the state provides mechanisms for economic 'planning' and coordination. Secondly, it provides or regulates inputs for the accumulation process, such as land supply or finance. Thirdly, it intervenes to maintain consensus by reducing 'the more disruptive effects of accumulation, including the prevention of pollution, degradation of land and townscape, or wide regional disparities'.[1] These functions vary in their importance according to the stage of the accumulation process. In a crisis, the third one, intervention for consensus, assumes less importance than the other two. The first two functions are performed by the state at other times than in a crisis, but they assume far more importance in a crisis when they concentrate on particular aspects of restructuring and adopt new forms of intervention such as shareholding.

Local and regional shareholding from 1966 was concerned with restructuring as part of the state's economic planning function. But involvement in restructuring was accompanied by attempts to protect the local economy from the disruptive effects of developments. Many of these attempts to control disruptive effects had their historical origins in the need to intervene to establish or protect consensus over issues, and there had been extensive discussions by local authorities during the 1960s and early 1970s about how to secure such objectives. There was also a history of regional policy which had been aimed at minimising the disruptive effects of regional unemployment disparities. We have described how the HIDB and NIFC began as developments of this policy. We have also described how in Shetland the local authority attempted to control the disruptive effects of oil developments, and how in Southend the Council was concerned about the disruptive effects of the third London airport. However, we have also described how all the local and regional authorities were concerned to facilitate development or investment as well, and how the policies of the HIDB and NIFC, as well as those of the local authorities in facilitating development, are concerned chiefly with securing profitable schemes or enterprises. In the case of the HIDB and NIFC only the original establishment of the regional agencies as 'special cases' can be seen as intervention for consensus. Their performance in providing equity is more consistent with the function of supplying vital inputs for firms which faced similar financial restructuring problems *regardless of their regional location*. In the case of the local authorities concerned with minimising disruptive effects and securing development, their performance is consistent with supplying inputs for development in a controlled way within strict financial limits. In other words, the maintenance of consensus has not disappeared but in relative terms it has assumed less importance than the financial restructuring and facilitation role of the state.

It was no coincidence that the need arose to support the existence of a local authority airport in the East Midlands and that at the same time passenger transport authorities sought mechanisms for raising additional finance for their operations, that local and regional authorities supported the growth of new firms, either connected with their existing functions or not, that development and speculation was influenced and controlled, and that an increasing involvement with the local economy came about. Shareholding was a mechanism which in a small way helped to secure a range of objectives which all arose out of the crisis. The importance of *shareholding* is its role as a tool of *managed intervention*, which has assumed growing importance during the crisis.

The pattern of local and regional authority shareholding reflects a particular role in a specific historical period of the accumulation process. This role consists of a set of responses to the three elements of the crisis we have discussed earlier:

(a) restructuring – attempts to secure the financial restructuring of small firms in an area and to develop new firms;

(b) property boom – the elimination of uncontrolled speculative development and its replacement by controlled facilitation, especially after the property boom had ended. This involved promoting a particular kind of development in which the private sector would not have invested by itself, securing a significant financial return from development and providing infrastructure for particular kinds of development;

(c) pressures to reduce public expenditure – attempts to continue local services by raising money elsewhere; to support firms and development projects as cheaply as possible.

The shareholding activities we have analysed should not be regarded as exceptional to the 'normal' functions of the state. The state has a small but continuing direct role in the production process. This has varied in importance over time and it has also varied according to the level of the state (i.e. central, regional or local) at which it has taken place. We have seen the historical importance of municipalisation, then nationalisation, and now of shareholding. We have argued that these various kinds of intervention have meant that the state functions as an individual capital in the accumulation process. It acts as an individual capital does because providing the *general* conditions for accumulation in the form of education, housing, and roads does not suffice. Indeed, in the present crisis we have seen how certain functions of state intervention, such as the maintenance of consensus, assume less importance than the restructuring of capital. In other words, as the state has performed more as an individual capital, the general conditions for accumulation which individual capitals themselves do not provide have assumed a relatively inferior importance. We would regard this direct role in accumulation as quite 'normal', although its *form* has changed over time because the problems of accumulation also change over time.

Other explanations of intervention at the level of the firm are inadequate because they ignore the specific historical functions which shareholding performs in the accumulation process. The 'quasi non-governmental organisations' argument, the 'overloaded government' argument and the 'corporatist' argument all fail to locate state intervention in relation to the dynamic of accumulation. State shareholding cannot be explained by the QUANGO argument as a response to the increasing 'complexity' of society. This is a vague argument based on the premise that there is no identifiable mode of production in Britain, but, rather, a 'confusing' system which is not capitalism. The QUANGO argument has probably tried to explain the existence of too many different types of institution. The result is a very general explanation in which QUANGOs are said to spread power, or to get round organisational weaknesses of traditional government, or to help organisations survive which could not do so without government support. In addition the QUANGO argument pays too much attention to the differences between public and private sector interests which give rise to problems of accountability. We have seen how the state has retained overall policy control in the case of shareholding and how there has been basic agreement between the state and the companies about the objective of the enterprises.

State shareholding cannot be seen, either, as a way of devolving power and reducing the 'overload' on government. It is indeed a 'partnership' between the public and private sector but it does not result from a need to find ways of simplifying complex issues, and reducing the responsibility on central government for complex and conflicting demands. The role of local and regional authorities is one where central government has only allowed a certain amount of 'devolution' of shareholding powers and has contained the pressures by local authorities for more devolution. Future developments in shareholding are likely to take place under central control, as we outline later. Shareholding is also not a matter of devolving some decision-making responsibility to the private sector. Instead state shareholding has increased the decision-making role of the state in economic planning and in the provision of land and financial inputs to accumulation in the crisis. According to the overloaded government thesis it might be argued that the state could have nationalised or municipalised, but that instead more of a partnership between the public and private sectors arose. However, state shareholding has not arisen because complete ownership and responsibility is too much of a burden. As we have explained, the institutional form of direct intervention in risk-taking through shareholding is appropriate to the accumulation crisis in which a restructuring of private capital is taking place. Nationalisation/municipalisation are appropriate to other periods when a longer-term control over the supply and pricing of certain basic materials becomes useful.

The corporatism argument contains a description of economic crisis but no theory of capitalism which it can use to justify its position. It implies that because the state has adopted a significantly different role in the present period, the mode of production has changed from capitalist accumulation to one based on 'success', 'order', 'unity', and 'nationalism'. These goals are said to be established by the state and subject to state control. They are therefore said to imply 'corporatism'.

Local and regional authority shareholding has been concerned with promoting profitability – improving the rate of profit in relation to capital employed. It has meant that local and regional authorities have acted as private capital does and are subject to the logic of the accumulation process. Both the state and private capital take part in the various cycles of the accumulation process and the relative importance of the functions of the state within it vary in their intensity *and in their form* from one period to another. It cannot be argued that the authorities have established their own goals which are different from the dynamic of this process just because the relative importance of state intervention for restructuring has increased as the crisis has progressed.

The state is not controlling the accumulation process. The state's role and influence is limited by the eventual return of the companies to complete private control or by the completion of the development projects. The state's role is also limited by the fact that it is dependent to a certain extent on party political control. The Labour Party has exhibited a greater propensity than the Conservative Party to respond to the crisis at the local and regional levels, as well as at the national level, by use of shareholding. This is consistent with the social democratic ideology of the Labour Party which first declared its intention to use shareholding in a systematic way at the national level in the early 1960s.[2]

The state is not a cohesive, monolithic, 'corporate' entity with its own motivating force. It is part of the accumulation process which includes conflicting and contradictory elements. The main contradiction for our analysis is the conflict between small and large firms which is revealed further when different levels of the state attempt to assist different sizes of enterprise. Central government encourages local authority shareholding for development and infrastructure provision, including transport; large firms are usually involved in these ventures. It discourages local authority shareholding for manufacturing and commercial purposes; small firms are usually involved in these ventures. Regional authority shareholding in small firms has been allowed by central government in certain areas and under strict budgetary controls. This helps to fulfil the limited need for a small firms' sector within an economy dominated by large firms.

Our analysis only involves a few firms, particularly at the local authority level. However, the pressure from local authorities to intervene in their local economies reached a very high level by the mid-1970s. This pressure has been contained in various ways by Parliament and central government. It is important to take into account these pressures from local government on central government in any analysis of the 'corporate' nature of the state. Local authorities will continue to develop an economic role regardless of central government. The institutional forms this role assumes over the next few years may change because of the conflicts between central and local government, but there seems little doubt that the function will develop further.

Our evidence about local and regional shareholding would not therefore support the contention that Britain was, or was becoming, corporatist. Our main points from this and earlier chapters are:

(a) state intervention at these levels is concerned with securing profitability for the individual firm and for capital as a whole;
(b) the intervention is limited in duration in each individual case and its importance is related largely to the crisis; where the intervention is

more prolonged the state's objectives are no different from the
dynamic of normal production;

(c) the intervention is limited by differences in party control;

(d) the intervention includes conflicts between the levels of the state
which stems from the conflicts between large and small enterprises;

(e) state enterprise at sub-national level is not new and has assumed
different forms in the past according to the functions being
performed: there is a great danger that the catchword for state
enterprise will no longer be 'municipal socialism' as it was 100 years
ago, but 'local corporatism'.

We have demonstrated how the specific functions of local and regional
authority shareholding are a response to aspects of the current crisis, but if
we are to estimate what role shareholding will perform in future we must
also consider the ability of these authorities to incorporate the shareholding mechanism into the existing planning process. Regional authority
shareholding by the HIDB and NIFC has generally been regarded as an
extension of national economic planning. First it was used for the 'special
cases' of the Scottish Highlands and Northern Ireland. These areas were
thought to require investment policies which were sensitive to the
particular regional problems of unemployment, distance from capital
markets and civil unrest. Later it was used for the more general financial
restructuring of industry. At the local authority level, however, shareholding is an entirely new mechanism, requiring a new role for local authorities
together with new or reinterpreted legal powers and provisions. At present
it does not fit easily into the 'planning' procedures laid down by the 1971
Town Planning Act. Planning is divided into two complementary
functions of plan- or policy-making on the one hand, and plan implementation or control on the other. In practice, these two functions are
separated too much for shareholding to be easily introduced because this
particular mechanism requires a closely integrated process of policy-
making and implementation. In addition, the introduction of the profit
motive into local authority activities has appeared a long period after the
decline of municipal trading. Many questions have consequently been
raised about the wisdom behind direct economic intervention, which is
regarded as the preserve of central government and now of regional
authorities too.

Town planning has traditionally been concerned with the allocation of
land for development and to a lesser extent with the effects of economic
processes on the population of a given area. Economic planning at the local
level has in most cases implied improving local employment opportunities
by means of attraction and location of industry and commerce. The
Development Plans manual[3] uses the terms 'employment', 'income',
'industry', and 'commerce' as suggested aspects for analysis and policy-

making in the structure plan, but these terms refer to the composition of the workforce, the distribution of jobs, the accessibility of jobs to work places and the availability of land, and not on the viability of the firm and industrial growth. Similarly, the 'location and scale of employment' is one of the three 'key issues' that the DoE have suggested structure plans should emphasise,[4] reinforcing the view that local government is concerned with 'consensus' objectives such as promoting employment, while central government operates with the economic planning objectives of facilitating and controlling private investment.

The town planning profession developed its ideological foundations mainly during the post-Second World War period when there was rapid population increase, economic growth, and widespread physical destruction caused by the war. Under these conditions notions of 'the public benefit' and 'social objectives' developed which were regarded as mostly in conflict with the profit-oriented objectives of the private sector. This is because the state was mainly performing a consensus role. The system of plan-making and development control kept the private entrepreneur at a distance, and any negotiations between the local authority and entrepreneur were regarded as a bargaining process within which 'social' benefits deriving from the objectives of public plans would be traded-off against private commercial objectives.

An examination of the traditional partnerships between the local authority and private sector demonstrate the nature of the town planning function that was used from the 1950s to the early 1970s. Throughout the period the national economy was growing and the state at the local level did not need to intervene directly in the accumulation process. To begin with, local authorities were concerned to provide the general conditions of accumulation. In competition with one another, they attracted investment with gifts or subsidies to the private sector, such as grants, loans, the waiving of rents, and the provision of land, buildings and infrastructure. Later, during the 1960s and early 1970s under boom conditions in the property industry and before the effects of the crisis had become apparent, local authorities continued to make these gifts, but concentrated on intervening to reduce the disruptive effects of large-scale private investment such as traffic congestion, noise and pollution. Whenever they were in a strong bargaining position they attempted to obtain 'planning gain' or modification to investment proposals which helped to reduce the most disruptive effects of developments. 'Planning gain' could be obtained through Section 52 bargains (1968 and 1971 Town Planning Acts), conditions attached to planning permissions, or by the much frowned-upon 'selling of planning permissions'. More recently, partnerships have reflected the slump in the property market and the general economic crisis. Where financial institutions have been unwilling to invest and where developers and industrialists have faced temporary financial difficulties, local authorities have formed a variety of partnerships which do not involve them in any risk and which are tailor-made to each particular circumstance, such as lease and leaseback, profit-sharing, or industrial mortgages.

All these partnerships involve the local authority either in trying to make its area more attractive for private investment by a gift or subsidy, providing the general conditions for accumulation, or in reducing the most disruptive effects of investment decisions, or in trying to claw back some private profits for itself. These aims need not be mutually exclusive. In each case, however, local economic planning is represented as a tug-of-war between opposed sets of public and private sector objectives, such as the promotion of local employment versus market tendencies to locate industry elsewhere.

As mechanisms for implementing plans these partnerships were negative and weak in that they were one-off agreements containing a rigidity not well suited to inflationary or unstable market conditions, and they depended on a degree of willingness by the private sector to invest. As well as attracting investment to a particular local authority area, they had the effect of lowering the costs of production and making the industry more competitive, but any 'planning gains' were generally fortuitous and dependent on general market conditions, the attractiveness of the particular site and the financial state of the firm concerned.

With these traditional partnerships the local authority has performed a different role from that which we have described earlier where shareholding has been used; as interventionist mechanisms the partnerships were aimed mainly at minimising the disruptive effects of the accumulation process, for instance, by locating industry separately from housing areas, or by locating new office development at the centre of public transport systems. However while consensus was promoted, planning encouraged the merger and takeover and the relocation of large firms within a process of concentration and centralisation of capital, and by default, the growth of small firms was discouraged.[5] Numerous attempts have been made by central government to improve the British local planning system over the last fifteen years in order to make it more relevant to local problems. There has been the 1965 Planning Advisory Group report,[6] the 1968 and 1971 Town and Country Planning Acts, the Community Land Act of 1976, more new towns programmes, the Bains and Paterson Reports, and growth in state expenditure and manpower. But the problem was seen as one of trying to achieve more consensus goals rather than to help in the restructuring of local firms and to increase local control. Also, they were central government-inspired changes which encouraged consensus goals such as 'public participation' which were irrelevant to local economic problems. It is hardly surprising that the traditional local planning system has failed utterly to deal with the local problems presented by the current crisis of general industrial decline, closure of small firms, loss of employment, near-stagnation of the property market, and the much-publicised inner city decay.

The shareholding schemes we have examined arose in response to aspects of the crisis as we have already shown, but equally important, they represent a transformation in the concept of planning within the historical development of the planning process in local government. The direct involvement of the local authority in the financial affairs of a company means the state's activities are an integral part of the accumulation process. There has been a progression from the traditional no-risk partnership to a situation where local and regional authorities have adopted a new financial role which involves them in the detailed operations of the firms concerned and the monitoring and influencing of their risk-taking activities (see Table 6.1). This progression has occurred in response to general economic conditions and has not taken place alongside parallel developments in the town planning profession.

TABLE 6.1 The development of partnerships in local planning

	Industry and Commerce	Development	Transportation
Risk-taking and continuous influence	shareholding	shareholding	shareholding
No-risk partnership	loans	returns as freeholder	
Influence	negative through planning permission and IDCs	discussion and agreemnts conditions for development at planning permission stage	operating agreements
Subsidies and gifts	factory space, grants, infrastructure and planning permission	land assembly, planning permission and infrastructure	stage-carriage and taking on of unprofitable activities

The same commercial objectives of the company are held by all the shareholders, including the state, and, as we have found, conflicts over major policy rarely arise between the public authority and the private company. This does not mean that the objectives of the state are the same as those of the private sector. While the state will aim to make a firm or project viable and profitable, the original decision to invest in a particular company is based on objectives which are different from those of a financial institution. The state's decision is affected by political pressures from sections of the population in response to factors such as high unemployment, and in many cases, the state will take a greater risk than the private sector would tolerate. The nature of this risk is the time it may take to make the company profitable, and the greater effort involved in investment and monitoring. Nevertheless, as we have shown, a commercial return on capital is expected in the long term. As a result the objectives of the local authority are framed within the dynamic of the company's operations: raising finance, production and marketing of commodities. They are more realistic than the objectives of the structure or local plan which are framed in the expectation that negotiations must take place between the local authority and the private sector and that only limited and unpredictable gains will be achieved.

Local authorities have been increasing their pressures on central government for wider shareholding powers to facilitate and control investment in their areas. Shareholding is regarded as a 'positive' planning mechanism and also one which is appropriate in a time of public expenditure restraint. Local authorities have been pressing for positive planning powers since the 1950s when the compensation and betterment provisions of the 1947 Town and Country Planning Act were removed. Since then the Land Commission was set up in 1967 but was quickly disbanded by the incoming Conservative Government. The Town and Country Planning Association promoted the idea of development agencies in 1974, and in 1975 the Community Land Act was passed which provided for land to be gradually brought under public ownership. However, hopes that this act would give 'teeth' to planning were short-lived; the provisions of the act have many 'exceptions' and 'exemptions', greatly reducing what is termed 'relevant development', and the 'use value' of land is so high in the centre of cities where the greatest need for public acquisition exists that local authorities cannot afford to buy it. More importantly, the public ownership of land does not necessarily make it attractive to private investors. A local authority-owned *company* operating on such land, however, is seen as one way of raising the private capital needed to facilitate development as well as controlling the type of development and recouping any profits made. Similarly, shareholding assists and controls the growth of small firms in manufacturing and commerce where other planning mechanisms are inappropriate. As well as being 'positive', shareholding also allows for continuous policy control through board membership or other monitoring procedures, and allows additional assistance to be given at the precise moment when it is needed.

The importance of shareholding to a local authority is its ability to stimulate investment, to control certain aspects of development, and to sustain the level of service provision within a crisis which involves public expenditure controls. Its potential as a planning mechanism is limited to the role it performs in the accumulation process so that an end to the present crisis would either make shareholding no longer useful, or else would change its function. There should be no pretence, as occurred with nationalisation and municipalisation, that shareholding has arisen for any other reason. In addition, if shareholding grows it must be seen in the context of a national economic and land-use policy. Otherwise there is a danger of an *ad hoc* growth in intervention which aggravates the existing competition and conflict between development areas and non-development areas, between inner-city and expanding town, between one tier of government and another, and between industries and development projects within a particular area.

Shareholding is likely to increase because equity is needed, and central government may have to integrate it into some form of national planning process in order to reconcile the conflicting needs of large and small firms over which central government will probably aim to exert ultimate control. Within such a national planning process the economic planning powers of local government, including powers to provide equity assistance, might be consolidated in a local authority planning institution, the Municipal Enterprise Board or some separate body which people have been pressing for. Central government would probably permit local authority MEBs to intervene in development because large companies are generally involved in the development process, and because managed intervention in land development has received bi-partisan acceptance since the property boom. However, shareholding in firms concerned with manufacture and commerce is likely to be controlled more tightly by central government as part of a wider process of managing the conflict between large and small firms.

This does not necessarily mean that central government itself will allocate resources to small firms; it is more likely that the function will be delegated to some regional authority which may also assume some of the strategic planning functions of local government. Nevertheless, in order to coordinate local and national planning policies, local authorities could be given a nominal shareholding and directorship in large companies in which the National Enterprise Board or the Scottish, Welsh and Northern Ireland Development Agencies, and any other regional agencies which are set up, have an interest. The regional authorities could also give equity and other financial support to small firms in the same sector as the large firms in which the NEB has shares, so that in the Midlands, for example, the regional authority might support engineering and motor car components and accessory firms while the NEB might support British Leyland. This would facilitate comprehensive, sectoral planning, investment and innovation, involving large and small firms in sectors of national economic importance, and it would facilitate a link between local land-use and national economic planning through the representation of local authority interests in companies in which the NEB or regional authorities have shares.

The 1968 Transport Act is a model of the kind of legislation which could be provided to allow Municipal or Regional Enterprise Boards similar sorts of powers to those of Passenger Transport Executives, but in specified industrial rather than transport activities. PTEs are the kind of mini-nationalised industry and holding company which MEBs or REBs could also become in that their distinct legal and financial basis in local government planning enables them to organise and administer their extensive service and trading responsibilities as a separate but related function within the rest of the authorities' responsibilities.

If local government, or some regional tier of government, were involved in this kind of economic planning process, sectoral planning would need to involve local and regional authority participation at the earliest stages. Central government would need to consult local and regional authorities affected by national plans to promote the growth of certain sectors in order to encourage local and regional authorities to use their assistance to industry powers in accordance with national priorities. Naturally there would be conflicts and contradictions in this state apparatus because the state is part of the accumulation process which contains those conflicts and contradictions. Increasing state intervention in industry will also be disliked by capital as a whole although, as we have found, individual firms react differently. When looked at in aggregate terms state shareholding represents a threat to the private ownership and control of the means of production, because private enterprise argues that the structure of state intervention can be 'misused' and the state 'captured' by socialism. Our analysis has shown that it has never been the case that state enterprise has been used this way, be it nationalisation, municipalisation, or state shareholding at any level. We have argued that the role of local and regional shareholding should always be considered in relation to different elements in the accumulation process and that it has a particular role to play in the present development of capitalism. When the nature of this role is appreciated local and regional authority shareholding can be used or controlled for what it is – a part of the role of the state in a crisis of capital accumulation.

Notes

Introduction
1 We use the word 'planning' for purposes of convenience. It is an imprecise term which can refer to most aspects of state intervention and not just economic and land-use 'planning'. Figure 1 is not therefore *the* 'planning' system. Henceforth 'planning' will not be in quotation marks and will refer to economic and land-use planning as appropriate.
2 *The Future of Development Plans* (HMSO, 1965).
3 W. Solesbury, *Policy in Urban Planning* (Pergamon Press, 1974).
4 P. Hall, *Urban and Regional Planning* (Penguin Books, 1974).
5 *Royal Commission on Local Government in England*, vol. 2, *Memorandum of Dissent* by D. Senior, Cmnd 4040–1 (HMSO, 1969); quoted in J. B. Cullingworth, *Town and Country Planning in Britain* (Allen & Unwin, 1972) p. 287.
6 Taken from Annual Reports, Parliamentary Debates and Discussion Documents.
7 S. Young and A. V. Lowe, *Intervention in the Mixed Economy* (Croom Helm, 1974).
8 D. C. Hague, W. J. M. Mackenzie and A. Barker (eds) *Public Policy and Private Interests – The Institutions of Compromise*, (Macmillan, 1975) pp. 13–18. Also, B. Smith (ed.) *The New Political Economy: The Public Use of the Private Sector* (Macmillan, 1975) and B. Smith and D. Hague (eds) *The Dilemma of Accountability in Modern Government* (Macmillan, 1973).
9 Hague, Mackenzie and Barker, op. cit., pp. 362–3.
10 Ibid., p. 13.
11 H. Seidman in Smith, op. cit., p. 83.
12 J. Douglas, 'The Overloaded Crown', *British Journal of Political Science*, 6, no. 4.
13 A. King, 'Overload: Problems of Governing in the 1970s', *Political Studies*, XXIII (1975).
14 See J. Cornford (ed.) *The Failure of the State* (Croom Helm, 1975) and Douglas, op. cit.
15 See R. E. Pahl and J. T. Winkler, 'The Coming Corporatism', *New Society* (10 October 1974); and J. T. Winkler, 'Corporatism', *European Journal of Sociology*, XVII (1976). The quotations in this section are taken from both these articles.

1 Intervention and the Crisis
1 K. Marx, *Capital*, vol. I (Lawrence & Wishart, 1974).
2 *Financial Times* (5 October 1976). Department of Industry figures.
3 *Economic Trends*, no. 263 (HMSO, September 1975); quoted in J. T. Winkler, 'Corporatism', *European Journal of Sociology*, XVII (1976).
4 Royal Commission on the Distribution of Income & Wealth, Report no. 2, Cmnd 6172 (HMSO, 1975) p. 77. The figures refer to large firms.

5 C. Johnson, *Anatomy of UK Finance, 1920–75* (Financial Times, 1976) p. 56.

6 Department of Industry, 1976.

7 G. Meeks and G. Whittington, 'Giant Companies in the UK, 1948–69', *Economic Journal*, 85 (December 1975) and *Royal Commission, on the Distribution of Income & Wealth*, op. cit.

8 *Banking and Finance* (The Labour Party, 1976).

9 *Trade and Industry* (5 December 1976).

10 *Committee of Inquiry on Small Firms* (The Bolton Report) Cmnd 4811 (HMSO, 1972 reprint).

11 ICFC's shareholders are the National Westminster Bank, Midland Bank, Barclays Bank, Lloyds Bank, the Royal Bank of Scotland, Williams & Glyn's Bank, the Bank of England, Clydesdale Bank, the Bank of Scotland, Coutts & Company.

12 The Bolton Report, research report no. 5; also *Royal Commission on the Distribution of Income and Wealth*, op. cit., para. 247.

13 S. J. Prais, *The Evolution of Giant Firms in Britain* (Cambridge University Press, 1976). Prais defines small firms as establishments with ten employees or less.

14 The Bolton Report.

15 G. Bannock, *The Smaller Business in Britain & Germany* (Wilton House, 1976) pp. 69–70.

16 M. Stewart, 'Labour and the Banks', *New Society* (23 September 1976).

17 Victor Keegan and Frances Cairncross, *Guardian*, (1 July 1976).

18 *Financial Times* (8 June 1976).

19 *Economist* (15 May 1976).

20 *Guardian* (9 March 1977).

21 The Bolton Report.

22 Adapted from N. Poulantzas, *Classes in Contemporary Capitalism* (New Left Books, 1975) pp. 142–3.

23 *Banking and Finance*, p. 14.

24 *Land*, Cmnd 5730 (HMSO, 1974) para 16.

25 J. Hughes, *Funds for Investment* (Fabian Research Series 325, 1976) p. 4.

26 Various figures from I. Gough, 'State Expenditure in Advanced Capitalism', *New Left Review*, no. 92.

27 P. Townsend and N. Bosanquet (eds), *Labour and Inequality* (Fabian Society, 1972).

28 M. Chisolm, 'Regional Policies in an Era of Slow Population Growth and Higher Unemployment', *Regional Studies*, vol. 10, no. 2 (1976) p. 202.

29 Evidence from Department of Employment to Trade and Industry Sub-Committee of the Expenditure Committee, *Regional Incentives* (HMSO, 1973/4).

30 D. Massey and R. Meegan, 'Industrial Restructuring versus the City', in A. Evans and D. Eversley (eds), *The Inner City Employment Problem* (forthcoming).

31 Ibid.

32 D. Massey, *Restructuring and Regionalism: Some Spatial Implications of the Crisis in the UK*, paper presented to North American Regional Science Association, November 1976: available from the Centre for Environmental Studies as CES Working Note 449.

33 O. Marriott, *The Property Boom* (Pan Books, 1969) p. 16.

34 Ibid.

35 Ibid.
36 *Investors Chronicle*, Property Investment Review (May, 1976).
37 M. Harrison, 'Town Centre Redevelopment', *Municipal and Public Services Journal* (21 June 1974).
38 G.Adams, 'The Highlands Dilemma', *New Society* (26 February 1976).
39 Scottish Standing Committee, Highlands Development Bill: First Sitting, March 1965, col. 20, M. Noble, M. P. for Argyll.
40 Ibid: Second Sitting, col. 96 Doig, M.P. for Dundee West.
41 Ibid: Third Sitting, col. 119.
42 NIFC, First Annual Report, 1972/3: our emphasis.
43 Scottish Standing Committee, Highlands & Islands Industry Bill, 8 May 1968 col. 17: R. Maclennan, M.P. for Caithness and Sutherland, one of the promoters of the Bill.
44 Ibid, col. 27 G. Campbell, M.P. for Moray and Nairn: our emphasis.
45 Department of the Environment, Report of Working Party on *Local Authority/Private Enterprise Partnership Schemes* (HMSO, 1972).
46 *Widening the Choice: the Next Steps in Housing* (HMSO, 1973).
47 Harrison, op. cit.
48 P. B. Rogers and C. R. Smith, 'The Local Authority's Role in Economic Development; the Tyne and Wear Act 1976', *Regional Studies*, vol. II, no. 3 (1977).
49 Council Minutes, 13 May 1975.
50 *Guardian* (3 March 1977); *Financial Times* (14 March 1977).
51 Standing Conference on London and South-East Regional Planning, *Strategy for the South-East; A Conference Response to Government* (February 1977).
52 Northern Region Strategy Team, *Strategic Plan for the Northern Region*, vol. 1, Main Report (HMSO, 1977).
53 The Royal Town Planning Institute, *Memorandum of Observations Submitted to the Department of the Environment on the Inner Area Studies* (March 1977).
54 West Midlands County Council, *Annual Economic Review*, no. 2 (March 1977).
55 *Guardian* (8 February 1977).
56 Ibid.
57 *Parliamentary Debates* (6 April 1977).

2 *Municipal Socialism or Local Capitalism*

1 T. Daintith, 'The Development of the Mixed Economy', in W. Friedmann (ed.) *Public and Private Enterprise in Mixed Economies* (Stevens, 1974).
2 G. N. Ostergaard, 'Labour and the Development of the Public Corporation', *Manchester School of Economic and Social Studies* (May 1954).
3 Daintith, op. cit.
4 B. Donoughue and G. W. Jones, *Herbert Morrison: Portrait of a Politician* (Weidenfeld & Nicholson, 1973) p. 145.
5 Daintith, op. cit.
6 H. Finer, *Municipal Trading* (Allen & Unwin, 1941).
7 E. J. Hobsbawm, *Industry and Empire* (Penguin Books, 1969).
8 Bentley B. Gilbert, *The Evolution of National Insurance in Britain: The Origins of the Welfare State* (Michael Joseph, 1966) pp. 33–8.
9 Ibid.

10 J. Harris, *Unemployment and Politics* (Clarendon Press, 1972) p. 209.
11 Finer, op. cit., p. 19.
12 Ibid, p. 25.
13 DoE, Welsh Office, Ministry of Agriculture, Fisheries and Food, *Review of the Water Industry in England and Wales* (HMSO, 1976).
14 *The Reorganisation of the Ports*, Cmnd 3903 (HMSO, 1969).
15 J. Tilley, *Changing Prospects for Direct Labour*, Fabian Tract 445, 1976.
16 West Midlands County Council Bill 1975, clause 5(c).
17 M. Barratt Brown, *Bulletin of the Institute of Workers Control*, no. 9 (1971).
18 W. Robson, *Nationalised Industry and Public Ownership* (Allen & Unwin, 1960).
19 S. Holland, *The Socialist Challenge* (Quartet Books, 1975) p. 67.
20 *Guardian* (4 April 1977).
21 Ibid.
22 S. Young and A. L. Lowe, *Intervention in the Mixed Economy* (Croom Helm, 1974).
23 Ibid.
24 W. Thornhill, 'Government Shareholdings', *Local Government Chronicle* (14 May 1976) p. 456.
25 Ibid.
26 Daintith, op. cit.
27 Ibid.
28 *The Times* (4 February 1977).
29 March Budget, 1977.
30 Daintith, op. cit.

3 Categorisation of Schemes
1 D. B. Chynoweth, 'CRIS – A New Venture for Superannuation Fund Investment', *Local Government Chronicle* (26 March 1976).
2 Ibid.
3 GLC Minutes, 25 May 1976.
4 Joint Planning Group of Oil Industry and Council, *Shetland Crude Oil Terminal: Overall Development Plan*.
5 Ibid.
6 *Shetland Times* (June 1975).

4 Manufacture and Commerce
1 See K. Midgley, 'How Much Control do Shareholders Exercise?', *Lloyds Bank Review*, no. 114 (October 1974).
2 *Admission of Securities to Listing* (The Stock Exchange, 1973 and updated).
3 Labour Research Department, *How to Get the Facts about Profits and Prices* (1975).
4 The information on rates of return for large companies was obtained from the *Investors Chronicle*, Company Analysis. The calculations are broadly similar to ours.
5 *Investors Chronicle*, Company Analysis (3 December 1976).
6 Ibid. (1 April 1977).
7 Ibid. (4 February 1977).
8 Ibid.
9 Ibid. (1 May 1977).

5 Land Development and Infrastructure
1 M. Jones and F. Godwin, *The Oil Rush* (Quartet Books, 1976).
2 Ibid.
3 Ibid., p. 128.
4 *Shetland Times* (9 April 1976).
5 Ibid.
6 SVEAG *Oil Terminal at Sullom Voe: Environmental Impact Assessment* (Thuleprint, May 1976).
7 *Shetland Times* (15 April 1977).
8 E. Thomason in *New Shetlander*, no. 114 (Yule 1975) p. 31.

6 Shareholding as Managed Intervention
1 R. Murray, *Multinational Companies and Nation States* (Spokesman Books, 1975) p. 64.
2 *Signposts for the 'Sixties* (The Labour Party, 1961).
3 DoE, *Development Plans – A Manual on Form and Content* (HMSO, 1970).
4 'Structure Plans', DoE Circular 98/74 (July 1974).
5 Regional policy operated in a similar way: see G. Wood, 'Why Small Firms Lose in the Fight for Grants', *Financial Times*, (8 May 1973).
6 *The Future of Development Plans* (HMSO, 1965).

Index

shareholding, 63–4, 87–90
in a proposed planning structure, 149
North Scottish Helicopters Ltd, 87
Norwich City Council, 69, 110–11, 113–16, 125–6
Nottinghamshire County Council, 66–7, 90, 97, 98, 107

Overloaded government, 10, 142

Partnership arrangements, 110, 145–6
Passenger transport authorities, 44
Pearson Green Ltd., 80, 134
Peterhead City Council
compared with Shetland, 112
Planning Advisory Group, 4–5, 146
Productive expenditure, 16
Productive labour, 16
Profit rates
fall in Britain, 17–18
local and regional authority companies, 99–108, 127–35
Property boom, 21–2
spatial implications, 26–8
Prudential Assurance Ltd, 69, 123
Public Corporation, 39, 47–9
Public dividend capital, 49, 53, 88
Public Health Act, 1848, 43
Public works, 45–6
programmes, 42

Quasi-non-governmental and quasi-governmental organisations (QUANGOs and QUAGOs), 9–10, 141–2

Regional Economic Planning Councils and Boards, 7
Regional Planning, 6–8
Regional Water Authorities, 44
Restructuring of capital, 17–21
spatial implications, 25–6
R. G. Carter (Developments) Ltd, 115, 133
Rio-Tinto-Zinc Investments Ltd, 77
Rothschild & Sons Ltd, 80
Royal Town Planning Institute, 33

Scottish Development Agency
and regional planning, 8
in a proposed planning structure, 149
Scottish Industrial Estates Corporation
and regional planning, 8
Scottish Sea Farms Ltd, 86
SELNEC Transport Services Ltd, 80, 124, 133
Shell (UK) Ltd

and Southend, 77
and Shetland, 130
Shetland Aggregates Ltd, 65, 90, 98, 107
Shetland Hotels Ltd, 106
Shetland Islands Council, 65–6, 77–9, 91, 112, 126, 130–2, 135
Shetland-Norse Ltd, 65, 90, 91, 98, 107
Shetland Towage Ltd, 121
Small firms
and crisis of accumulation, 19–21
South Glamorgan County Council, 32
South Yorkshire County Council, 68
South Yorkshire PTE, 67, 98
Southend Borough Council, 76–7, 113
Special directors
and HIDB, 95–6
and NIFC, 97
Standing Conference on London and South-East Regional Planning, 33
State enterprise
definition of 38–40
State expenditure
controls 22–4, 28
Strategic Plan for the Northern Region, 33
Sullom Voe Association, 78, 81, 117–19, 126, 127, 130–2
Sullom Voe Environmental Advisory Group, 118–19
Surplus-value, 15–17

Thames Estuary Development Co. Ltd, 122–33
Thaneway Ltd, 86
Town and City Properties Ltd
Manchester development, 69, 123
Earls Court, 75
Southend development, 77
Town and Country Planning Act, 1947, 4, 148
Town and Country Planning Act, 1968, 4, 145, 146
Town and Country Planning Association, 148
Trafalgar Square riot, 1886, 42
Transport Act, 1968, 44, 149
Transport planning, 6
Tyne and Wear County Council, 32
Rapid transit system, 79
Tyne and Wear PTE, 79, 80, 124
Tyneside Transport Services Ltd, 80, 124, 133–4

Unemployed Workmen Act, 1905, 42

Water Act, 1973, 44
Welsh Development Agency
  and regional planning, 8
  in a proposed planning structure, 149
Welsh Industrial Estates Corporation
  and regional planning, 8
West Midlands County Council
  economic policy, 33
  private bill, 46

Horizon Midlands Ltd, 66
West Midlands Passenger Transport Ltd,
  124, 134
West Midlands PTE, 80, 124
West Yorkshire PTE, 67, 98
Whitbread & Co. Ltd, 80

Zetland County Council Act, 65, 77
Zetland Finance Ltd, 65